Second Edition

Improving
Test
Performance
of
Students
With
Disabilities

Second Edition

Improving Test Performance

of

Students With Disabilities

...On District and State Assessments

Judy L. Elliott ▪ Martha L. Thurlow

CORWIN PRESS
A SAGE Publications Company
Thousand Oaks, California

For information:

 Corwin Press
A Sage Publications Company
2455 Teller Road
Thousand Oaks, California 91320
www.corwinpress.com

Sage Publications Ltd.
1 Oliver's Yard
55 City Road
London EC1Y 1SP
United Kingdom

Sage Publications India Pvt. Ltd.
B-42, Panchsheel Enclave
Post Box 4109
New Delhi 110 017 India

Printed in the United States of America

Library of Congress Cataloging-in-Publication Data

Elliott, Judy L.
Improving test performance of students with disabilities . . . on district and state assessments / Judy L. Elliott, Martha L. Thurlow.— 2nd ed.
        p. cm.
Includes bibliographical references and index.
ISBN 1-4129-1727-1 (cloth) — ISBN 1-4129-1728-X (pbk.)
    1. Educational tests and measurements—United States. 2. Children with disabilities—Education—Ability testing—United States. 3. Education and state—United States. I. Thurlow, Martha L. II. Title.
LB3051.E48 2006
371.9'043—dc22

                                    2005009908

This book is printed on acid-free paper.

05   06   07   10   9   8   7   6   5   4   3   2   1

Acquisitions Editor:	Kylee Liegl
Editorial Assistant:	Jamie Cuvier
Production Editor:	Denise Santoyo
Typesetter:	C&M Digitals (P) Ltd.
Indexer:	Pamela Van Huss
Cover Designer:	Rose Storey
Graphic Designer:	Lisa Miller

Contents

Figures and Reproducible Forms

Preface

As we put the final touches on the revision of this book and it heads to print, the 2004 reauthorization of the Individuals with Disabilities Education Act (IDEA) had just been signed. Although no major changes were made to the assessment or instruction requirements in IDEA 2004, many states, districts, and schools were still adjusting to significant requirements that were added to IDEA in 1997. Among the 1997 amendments were those that required students with disabilities to have access to the general education curriculum (including the standards that are driving the curriculum); that required districts and states to include students with disabilities in state and districtwide assessments, with accommodations where appropriate; and that an alternate assessment be used with those students unable to participate in the regular state and district assessments. Furthermore, states were required to report the number of students taking state and district assessments and the number taking the alternate assessment. They also were required to report on the performance of students with disabilities in both types of assessments.

Little did we know that when the No Child Left Behind (NCLB) Act was signed into law by President George W. Bush in January 2002, such tremendous changes would occur in so little time for the accountability for student learning, including for the learning of students with disabilities. And as a result, the nation was forced to address the issue of how to make sure that students with disabilities actually benefit from their instruction—with the benefit shown on the assessment and ultimately reflected in the districts' and states' accountability systems.

IDEA 2004 made clear that students with disabilities are to be in the NCLB accountability system. Thus we need to know how students with disabilities are performing, and we need to expect that their performance will improve over time. Our discussions with many teachers, parents, and administrators, however, suggest to us that it is not obvious how to make sure that the performance of students with disabilities does increase.

We revised this book in our continued effort to address the need to work systematically to close the achievement gap and hence improve the test performance of students with disabilities. Of course, we do this with the belief that improving test performance translates into improved learning. In fact, we direct our suggestions toward ways to improve students' learning and performance on a variety of tasks, not just test taking.

AUDIENCE

This book was written to be a resource to all district and school professionals, particularly those overseeing programs for students with disabilities and other special needs students, including students who are English language learners, and the individuals responsible for instructing these students. As with our previous book, we hope that state-level personnel, as well as higher education teacher preparation personnel, will read this book, even though it is directed primarily toward educators in schools. Because the education of our children—all children—is a shared responsibility, we also address parents as we suggest how to improve the performance of students with disabilities.

OVERVIEW

We organized this book to take you step by step through some approaches to improving the performance of students with disabilities. As we do this, we provide you with lots of materials that you can use to help you make decisions, document what you have done, and keep track of student progress. In each chapter we provide you with a list of additional resources that might be helpful to you, as well as a list of Internet sites with information on the topic of the chapter.

To further your use of and thinking on the contents of the chapters, we have provided you an opportunity via *Reflections on Change* to assess where your own knowledge and comfort are with each topic covered in the book. You will find this in Appendix A in the book.

We have created a list of technical assistance and dissemination networks that can provide information relevant to the topics covered in this book. Some of them are national resources; others are regional.

We have made every attempt to develop a book that is very usable, with both information and strategies and materials to support both. We hope that as you use this book, you will provide us with feedback on its usefulness in meeting your needs and in improving student performance.

Acknowledgments

This book takes us to the next logical step from where we were when we completed the second revision of the book, *Testing Students with Disabilities: Practical Strategies for Complying with District and State Requirements.* It is a book that begged to be written, because as states and districts began to include students with disabilities, it became clear that they often were not well-equipped for the experience. They needed both test-taking skills and the content-based instruction that are so often taken for granted.

We thank those individuals who took the time to review the text for us. They are Ron Felton, Associate Superintendent, Miami-Dade School District; Chris Dominguez, Assistant Superintendent, Office of Curriculum, Instruction, and Professional Development, Long Beach Unified School District; and Thomas Hehir, Director, School Leadership Program, Harvard University.

Judy L. Elliott
Martha L. Thurlow

In addition, Corwin Press would like to thank the following reviewers:

Gary P. McCartney, Superintendent
Portland School District, Allentown, PA

Susan Lagos, Clinical Associate Professor
University of Iowa, Iowa City, IA

Joan Henley, Assistant Professor
Arkansas State University, State University, AR

Margaret J. McLaughlin, Professor and Associate Director,
Department of Special Education
University of Maryland, College Park, MD

Susan M. Danmiller, Director of Special Education and Public Services
School District of Grafton, Grafton, WI

Jo-Anne Goldberg, Child Study Team
Mainland Regional High School, Linwood, NJ

Benjamin O. Canada, Associate Executive Director, District Services
Texas Association of School Boards, Austin, TX

About the Authors

Judy Elliott, PhD, is Assistant Superintendent of Special Education in the Long Beach Unified School District, Long Beach, California. Formerly Research Associate at the National Center on Educational Outcomes, she worked and continues to assist districts and state education departments in their efforts to update and realign curriculum frameworks, instruction, and assessments to include all students. Her research interests focus on effective instruction and Individualized Education Program (IEP) development and its alignment with standards and assessment; IEP team decision making for accountability, accommodation, and assessment; as well as translating information on standards and assessment for various audiences including parents, teachers, school boards both local and state, and other community groups. Elliott serves as a national consultant and staff development professional to state departments of education, school districts and organizations. She has trained thousands of staff, teachers, and administrators, both in the South Pacific and United States, in areas of leadership; inclusive schooling including linking assessment to classroom intervention; strategies and tactics for effective instruction; curriculum modification for students with mild to significant disabilities; intervention and teacher assistance teams; authentic and curriculum-based evaluation; prevention-intervention techniques; strategies for difficult-to-manage students; collaborative teaching; program evaluation; and accountability and assessment practices. Elliott has served as a consultant on several federal consent decrees, legislative panels and committees, advisory boards, and national research projects.

Some of her most recent cowritten books are *Strategies and Tactics for Effective Instruction-II, Timesavers for Educators,* and *Testing Students With Disabilities: Practical Strategies for Complying With State and District Requirements* (2nd ed.).

Martha Thurlow, PhD, is Director of the National Center on Educational Outcomes. In this position, she addresses the implications of contemporary U.S. policy and practice for students with disabilities, as well as English-language learners with disabilities, including national and statewide assessment policies and practices, standards-setting efforts, and graduation requirements. Thurlow has conducted research involving special education for the past 35 years in a variety of areas, including assessment and decision making, learning disabilities, early childhood education, dropout prevention, effective classroom instruction, and integration of students with disabilities in general education settings. During the past decade, she has been the principal investigator on 15 federal or state projects that have focused on the participation of students with special needs in large-scale assessments, with particular emphasis on how to obtain valid, reliable, and comparable measures of the knowledge and skills of these students while at the same time ensuring that the assessments are truly measuring their knowledge and skills rather than their disabilities or limited language when these are not the focus of the assessment. Recent research has focused on strategies to support the achievement of students. Thurlow has published extensively on all of these topics on which she has conducted research. She has also presented at numerous state, regional, national, and international conferences. She has testified before Congress on the inclusion of students with disabilities in accountability systems, and is often called upon by individuals at all levels of the educational system to provide input on challenging issues surrounding the inclusion of special needs students. In 2003, Thurlow completed an eight-year term as coeditor of *Exceptional Children*, the research journal of the Council for Exceptional Children. She is the coauthor of several books, including *Critical Issues in Special Education* (3rd ed.) and *Testing Students With Disabilities: Practical Strategies for Complying With State and District Requirements* (2nd ed.).

Maximizing the Performance of Students With Disabilities

From a little spark may burst a mighty flame.

—Dante

An accountability system is needed for all students and at the broadest level should apply to all students regardless of their characteristics.

—Jim Ysseldyke

Hot-Button Issues

- Whatever happened to "educate the best, forget about the rest"?
- Are we not kidding ourselves when we say that all students can learn?
- All of this is more work than it is worth, right?

Is your school a *needs-improvement* school? Have you met your adequate yearly progress (AYP) goals? What subgroup did not make AYP? These are the types of questions that are probably swirling around your current career as an educator—questions that just a few years ago would not have emerged from anyone's lips. They are questions about how well students are performing in school. Behind each of these questions is another question about what is to be done when accountability goals are not met. And, more to the point, how are certain groups of students, such as those with disabilities, ever going to show the performance that is needed for schools to be successful?

You have probably heard the phrase "all students can learn." Many schools, districts, and states have this phrase as part of their mission statements. More and more often, this phrase is now being followed by the phrase "all means all." Also, federal law and state and district policies are clarifying that the *all* in "all means all" includes students who have disabilities, as well as students who are English language learners. For some time, both of these groups were excluded from assessments and accountability systems—but no longer.

Federal and state laws now make it quite clear that all students—and that *all* includes students with disabilities—must be able to reap the benefits of a standards-based education. With the reauthorization of the Individuals with Disabilities Education Act in 1997 (IDEA 97), it became clear that students who have disabilities are to be included in state and districtwide assessments and that their performance is to be reported in a public way for all to see. The 2001 reauthorization of the Elementary and Secondary Education Act, known as the No Child Left Behind (NCLB) Act, supported these requirements and went a step further. NCLB placed the words *accountability* and *adequate yearly performance* on the lips of educators everywhere and on the lips of the public as well. This law requires not only that students participate in assessment systems but also that their scores be included in the NCLB accountability system, which produces AYP benchmarks for students overall and for each subgroup of students. The group of students with disabilities is one of those subgroups. The reauthorization of IDEA 97 in 2004, called the Individuals with Disabilities Education Improvement Act of 2004 (IDEA 2004), confirmed the participation of students with disabilities in the AYP accountability requirements.

The key elements of IDEA 97 and NCLB have created a whirlwind of activities in schools, districts, and states. To a large extent, the whirlwind reflects a need to respond to some very new and innovative requirements— access to the general curriculum, participation in state and district assessments, public reporting of disaggregated results of students with disabilities, development of alternate assessments for those students unable to participate in regular assessments, accountability that requires targeting AYP toward a goal of 100% of students proficient by 2014 (all students and each subgroup), and a cap on the percentage of students in an alternate assessment who can demonstrate proficiency based on alternate achievement standards. A pending regulation at the time this book was written would allow for alternate assessment based on modified achievement standards. Both IDEA and NCLB had dramatic effects in their own ways for students with disabilities—essentially putting them on the educational radar of all! Box 1.1 provides more details on some of the critical assessment and accountability features of IDEA and NCLB.

An unintended consequence of the federal laws in some locations has been a jump to "game" the system. Can we move students with disabilities from one school to another so that there are not enough to count toward (or against) AYP goals? Why don't we encourage a few really poorly performing students to stay home from school because we still have enough flexibility in the 95% participation requirement to not have them participate? Questions about changing standards or assessments have been seriously discussed at the state level. In some places, there was successful avoidance for a long time of what needed to

Box 1.1

Key Elements of IDEA 97, NCLB, and IDEA 2004

Individuals With Disabilities Education Act of 1997 (IDEA 97)

Access to General Curriculum—Students with disabilities must have access to, participate in, and make progress in the general education curriculum; they also must receive the services, supports, accommodations, and adaptations to ensure their participation and progress.

Participation in State and Districtwide Assessments—Students with disabilities are to participate in state and districtwide general assessments, with appropriate accommodations where needed.

Develop Alternate Assessments—States are to develop alternate assessments for those students who cannot participate in general assessments given by states or districts.

Public Reporting of Results—Whenever the state publicly reports data on students without disabilities, it is required to also report disaggregated data on students with disabilities, including the number participating in the general assessment and their performance and the number participating in the alternate assessment and their performance.

No Child Left Behind Act

Adequate Yearly Progress (AYP)—Each state is to define the annual progress targets and benchmarks that indicate adequate yearly progress to move all students from their performance levels in 2001–2002 to 100% proficient in the year 2014. These targets must be met by all students overall, as well as by each subgroup of students.

Subgroups—Groups of students targeted for attention in the No Child Left Behind (NCLB) accountability system include ethnic and minority groups, low socioeconomic groups, English language learners (students with limited English proficiency), and students with disabilities.

95% Participation—Schools and districts must demonstrate that 95% of their student population and each subgroup participated in the assessment to meet AYP, regardless of performance levels. Low participation rates automatically throw schools into the "needs-improvement" or "not meeting AYP" category. Participation rates may be averaged across two or three years to obtain the 95% (the current year and one or two previous years). In addition, students who were unable to take an assessment during the testing window because of a significant medical emergency (such as a car accident) do not have to be counted against the participation rate.

1% Cap on Proficient Alternate Assessments Based on Alternate Achievement Standards—Although as many students as appropriate may participate in an alternate assessment based on alternate achievement standards (for students with significant cognitive disabilities), only up to 1% of the scores that are proficient or above will count toward AYP accountability measures; the remainder will fold into the below basic or equivalent category.

Individuals With Disabilities Education Improvement Act of 2004 (IDEA 2004)

Accommodations—Guidelines are to be developed for the provision of appropriate guidelines by the state (or for districtwide assessments, by the local educational agency). The state

(Continued)

(Continued)

(or district, for district assessments) must report to the public the number of children with disabilities who were provided accommodations in order to participate in regular assessments.

Alternate Assessments—Requirements for these assessments include that they are (1) aligned with the state's challenging academic content standards and challenging student academic achievement standards, and (2) measure the achievement of students with disabilities against alternate academic achievement standards if the state has adopted them. A pending NCLB regulation at the time this book was written that would allow for alternate assessments based on modified achievement standards is not addressed in IDEA 2004.

Universal Design—States and districts shall use universal design principles to the extent feasible in developing and administering any assessments.

be discussed—where the rubber hits the road— that is, the alignment of the curriculum and instruction with the standards and the assessments. Are students being taught what they need to be taught? Are students being prepared for the test? This book is about where the rubber meets the road.

The assumptions on which IDEA and NCLB are based are clear and sound. Even if we do not agree with exactly how the laws are being carried out, the assumptions ring loud and clear and are ones that underlie the contents of this book. Box 1.2 summarizes the assumptions and gives a brief explanation of each. It is well worth taking the time to read these and to challenge yourself about your beliefs and your practices. Do they align with the assumptions in Box 1.2?

This chapter is a preview of the chapters in this book—each of which is devoted to ways to improve the achievement and test performance of students who have disabilities. The tests that are the focus here are those that are used by states and districts to report on what students know and can do and, increasingly, to determine significant consequences for schools (such as school awards, school accreditation, and other NCLB-related sanctions) and for students (such as promotion from one grade to another and graduation from high school). Because students who have disabilities generally were not included in these kinds of assessments in the past, we have not necessarily examined how to make sure that when they sit down for a test or when they engage in a performance event—or when they put together a portfolio—that they will perform their best, or that their performance will be an accurate reflection of what they know and what they can do.

The goal of this book is to help you, as an educator, improve the achievement and test performance of each and every student who has a disability. We are confident that the suggestions in this book also can be of benefit to other students, but we suspect that many of the things that we suggest are already being used by other students—either because someone has already implemented them or because the students themselves have picked them up on their own.

Box 1.2

Assumptions About Including Students With Disabilities

Assumption 1: All children can learn.

This seemingly simple statement is at the core of the concept of including all students in educational accountability systems. It contains a recognition that all learning is important. It also encompasses an understanding of the dramatic effects that expectations can have on the learning of individuals and the need to be aware of a tendency to hold inappropriate expectations for individual children, particularly those who are performing below the level of other children who are the same as them in one way or another.

Assumption 2: Schools are responsible for the learning of all children.

A strong premise underlying American public education is that schools are a mechanism to bring equality to all children, regardless of background. Over time, policymakers have recognized that individuals who have disabilities are people first, and have the same rights as other citizens. Although it has taken some strong public laws to ensure that these rights are recognized and upheld, these rights remain an integral part of the assumptions underlying an inclusive accountability system.

Assumption 3: Whenever children are counted, all children must count.

To have an inclusive educational accountability system, students who have disabilities must count in the same way as other children. Not all students have to take the same test to be counted, but they must count. Special approaches may have to be taken to ensure that scores are comparable in agreed-upon ways, and these approaches must be decided on up-front with stakeholders talking to each other. But the bottom line is that all students must count—no ifs, ands, or buts.

Resources on the Assumptions for Including Students With Disabilities in Accountability

McDonnell, L. M., McLaughlin, M. J., & Morison, P. (1997) (Eds.). *Educating one & all: Students with disabilities and standards-based reform.* Washington, DC: National Academy Press.

Heubert, J., & Hauser, R. (1999) (Eds.). *High stakes: Testing for tracking, promotion, and graduation.* Washington, DC: National Academy Press.

Thurlow, M. L., Elliott, J. L., & Ysseldyke, J. E. (2003). *Testing students with disabilities: Practical strategies for complying with district and state requirements.* Thousand Oaks, CA: Corwin.

Elmore, R., & Rothman, R. (1999). *Testing, teaching, and learning: A guide for states and school districts.* Washington, DC: National Academy Press.

INCORPORATING STANDARDS INTO ASSESSMENT AND INSTRUCTION

A critical sequence must be followed if the achievement of students who have disabilities is to improve. The first and most basic step is to know the standards the student is supposed to be working toward and the nature of the assessment for these standards. This process involves doing some background work to really understand what is expected of students in the educational system.

Another critical step is ensuring that the student's instruction is directed toward those standards. This alignment must be addressed in the student's Individualized Education Program (IEP). No longer can IEPs be devoted only to what special education or related services will provide to the student. Instead, the IEP must address access to the general education curriculum and clarify how this is to occur.

Understanding what is needed to ensure that IEPs address standards is the focus of Chapter 2. Beyond this topic, the chapter clarifies how the IEP can be related to standards and instruction and how standards can be backmapped to the IEP. Then, all of this material is linked to what happens in the classroom, the home, and the community.

USING DATA TO DRIVE ASSESSMENT AND INSTRUCTION

There are many decisions that are made in attempts to improve students' achievement and performance on assessments. It is no longer reasonable for educators to make these decisions in the absence of data. In fact, it is essential to examine large-scale assessment data and other progress-monitoring data to make decisions about instruction and assessment for students with disabilities. Chapter 3 addresses several ways in which educators can collect and disaggregate (separate out) data to inform the instructional and assessment decision-making processes for students with disabilities.

MAKING GOOD DECISIONS ABOUT ACCOMMODATIONS

We know that many students with disabilities use accommodations when they participate in assessments. The right for students to have needed accommodations is guaranteed by law. Making good decisions about what accommodations are needed is an important part of ensuring that students really demonstrate knowledge and skills.

Many kinds of accommodations exist, and many specific accommodations might be selected for an individual student. We know that it is easy to overaccommodate students who have disabilities (i.e., identifying more than they need or will use). This situation is not helpful. Accommodations are not best selected by knowing the category of the student's disability. Making decisions in the past has often been no more than guesswork.

Student learning can be improved by making good decisions about needed accommodations. How this task can be done is the focus of Chapter 4. Decision-making tools are provided, in addition to ways to help students identify the accommodations that they will need in various instructional and assessment situations.

HELPING THE STUDENT PREPARE FOR TESTING

Test preparation is an overlooked aspect of improving test performance of students with disabilities. Many test-preparation skills are not even identified as critical, because they come naturally to students who do not have disabilities. These skills are test-taking strategies that are beneficial for all students; however, many of these strategies do not appear in typical test-preparation books. These strategies and other helpful hints are the focus of Chapter 5.

As with accommodations, the ultimate goal is to have the students eventually take over responsibility for test preparation. Thus, Chapter 5 also addresses how to help the students know what they must do to be prepared for a test and perform well on the test. These strategies will not be the same for every student. Therefore, educators must learn what specific strategies will be useful for individual students who have disabilities.

ADDRESSING THE NEEDS OF IEP/ELLs

Students with disabilities are students just like all other students. They are rich and poor, they come from many different ethnic groups, and they also may be English language learners (ELLs). As we continue to emphasize that we are talking about improving the achievement and test performance of all students with disabilities, we may have to give special consideration to students with disabilities who are ELLs. Increasingly, schools are faced with the reality of a rapidly changing clientele. More and more often, educators are working with students who might speak a different language, who might or might not be literate in their first language, who might or might not have ever been exposed to a written language, and who might or might not ever have been in an educational setting before. The special considerations that are to be given to these students are discussed in Chapter 6. They do not involve excluding these students from assessment and accountability systems, but instead involve thinking specifically about how we can best meet their instructional and assessment needs. We should be making decisions about their access to the general education curriculum, the accommodations that they receive, and how best to assess them in ways that do not simply give us a measure of their disability or their limited English skills.

IMPROVING TEST PERFORMANCE ON THE GENERAL ASSESSMENT THROUGH INSTRUCTION

We can do many surface-level things to improve the test performance of students with disabilities—we have been talking about some of these when we address test preparation, and to some extent when we discuss accommodations. There is a much deeper issue that needs to be addressed whenever we talk about improving achievement and performance on an assessment. In the same way that we addressed improved performance on the alternate assessment, we can only address improved performance on the general assessment by stepping back and talking about (and doing something about) instruction. Chapter 7 digs into instruction, highlighting what needs to be done to ensure that instruction is on target for improved performance. In addition, in this chapter there are ideas about how to deal with a thorny issue—what about those students who do not seem to fit into the instructional or assessment system well—the *gray area students*? Is instruction the solution for these students who so challenge the assessment system?

IMPROVING PERFORMANCE ON ALTERNATE ASSESSMENTS THROUGH INSTRUCTION

A small percentage of all students will participate in alternate assessments, based on alternate achievement standards—that is, assessments for students with significant cognitive disabilities. The development of alternate assessments was a new requirement when IDEA was reauthorized in 1997, so these assessments are still evolving. Nevertheless, students with disabilities with significant cognitive disabilities are required to participate in them, and their performance is included in NCLB measures of AYP for accountability purposes. As we think about improving the achievement and test performance of students with disabilities, we must realize that we also have to pay attention to improving the performance of students with disabilities who participate in alternate assessments. This is new thinking—first recognizing that these children can learn, then determining how to best ensure that they are learning, and finally ensuring that the expectations held for them are appropriately high. Chapter 8 looks at those students who participate appropriately in the alternate assessment based on alternate achievement standards, providing both a brief explanation of the nature of the assessment system and their inclusion in accountability and strategies for ensuring that the best decisions are made for these students to show improved performance on alternate assessments.

GENERATING PARENT/GUARDIAN SUPPORT—AND THE SUPPORT OF OTHERS, TOO

"It takes a village to raise a child," said former First Lady, and current Senator, Hillary Rodham Clinton, quoting an African proverb. Likewise, more than a single teacher is needed to improve the test performance of students—particularly students who have disabilities. We all know that the support of parents is important in efforts to improve students' test performance. Of course, if parental support cannot be obtained, we can still do much more. We believe, however, that there are many ways to gain parental support that take a minimal amount of effort but are tremendously helpful.

When we talk about parent/guardian support, we really should take a broad view and talk about family support. Siblings, aunts, uncles, grandparents—whoever might be available—can contribute to efforts to improve the test performance of students who have disabilities. Generating support among a larger group of people is helpful as well, including other individuals in the school (e.g., the office secretary, school nurse, or counselor) and people and resources in the community.

Critical steps in gaining parental and family support for improving the achievement and test performance of students who have disabilities are provided in Chapter 9. In addition, the chapter gives the educator and family ideas about additional resources that are available to help in the effort to improve test performance.

SUMMARY

Each of the chapters in this book provides a discussion and lots of resources for you to take into your school. To help you be sure that you are taking away the important points from the chapter, we provide a set of "Hot-Button Issues" at the start of each chapter and a "Test Your Knowledge" set of questions at the end.

After every few chapters, we present a personal survey to use to determine where you stand in relation to the information that has been presented thus far in the book. At the end of this book are Appendix A, "Reflections on Change," and Appendix B, "Technical Assistance and Dissemination Networks," which contains technical assistance networks to support you as you work to improve achievement and test performance.

TEST YOUR KNOWLEDGE

Just to be sure that you have a general idea of what we hope to achieve in this book, complete the following fill-in-the-blank statements. Do not hesitate to reread parts of this chapter if the words that go in the blanks do not jump immediately into your head.

1. The phrases "all students can learn" and "all means all" include students who have _____ and students who are _____ language learners.

2. Federal laws require students who have disabilities to be included in state and districtwide assessments and require their performance to be _____.

3. The chapters in this book are devoted to ways to _____ the achievement and test performance of students who have disabilities.

4. IEPs must address _____.

5. It is essential to examine large-scale assessment and other progress monitoring _____ to make decisions about instruction and assessment for students with disabilities.

6. Student performance can be improved by making good decisions about needed _____.

7. One goal is to have the students take over responsibility for test _____.

8. We have to pay attention to improving the _____ of students with disabilities who participate in alternate assessments.

9. We can only address improved performance on the general assessment by talking about (and doing something about) _____.

10. When we talk about parental support, we really should be broader and talk about _____ support.

Box 1.3

While we will not repeat this material in each chapter, you might want to apply a scoring rubric each time you test your knowledge. Something like the following scoring guide would work.

How Did You Do? Use the Scoring Guide Below:

- 8–10 Way to go!
- 6–7 Getting there.
- 5–6 Moving in the right direction.
- 4–5 Reread the chapter again.
- 2–3 Uh-oh.
- 1–2 Not Yet!

ANSWERS

1. disabilities; English (p. 2)

2. reported (p. 2)

3. improve (p. 4)

4. standards (p. 6)

5. data (p. 6)

6. accommodations (p. 6)

7. preparation (p. 7)

8. performance (p. 8)

9. instruction (p. 8)

10. family (p. 8)

RECOMMENDED RESOURCES

McDonnell, L. M., McLaughlin, M. J., & Morison, P. (Eds.). (1997). *Educating one & all: Students with disabilities and standards-based reform.* Washington, DC: National Academy Press.

Thurlow, M., Elliott, J., & Ysseldyke, J. (2003). *Testing students with disabilities: Practical strategies for complying with district and state requirements (2nd ed.).* Thousand Oaks, CA: Corwin.

U.S. Department of Education. (2002). *No Child Left Behind: A desktop reference.* Washington, DC: Office of Elementary and Secondary Education. (available at www.ed.gov/NCLB)

U.S. Department of Education. (2004, rev.). *No Child Left Behind: A toolkit for teachers.* Washington, DC: Office of Elementary and Secondary Education. (available at www.ed.gov/NCLB)

U.S. House Committee on Education & the Workforce. (2004). *Frequently asked questions about No Child Left Behind* (updated April 1, 2004). Washington, DC: Author.

INTERNET RESOURCES

Council for Exceptional Children: www.cec.sped.org/

National Center for Research on Evaluation, Standards, and Student Testing: cresst96 .cse.ucla.edu/index.html

National Center on Educational Outcomes (NCEO): www.nceo.info

National Dissemination Center for Children with Disabilities (NICHCY): www.nichcy. org

Office of Elementary and Secondary Education (OESE): www.ed.gov/oese

Standards-Based Assessment and Instruction

Excellence for a few, but not for you.

—Anonymous

If you treat students as they are, they become worse. If you treat them as they could be, they become better.

—Gerald Tirozzi

Hot-Button Issues

- Why do all students need to work toward the same standards, anyway?
- Linking the Individualized Education Program (IEP) to standards is just more busywork.
- What has happened to the "I" in IEP?
- I have a stack of standards on my desk! I have no idea what to do with them!

So what is all the noise about standards, anyway? And why do parents, teachers, and administrators need to know about them?

The backbone of educational accountability is the evaluation of how students, including students who have disabilities and those who have limited English proficiency, are learning and progressing in today's schools. How can we really account for student learning if we do not have a common measure by which to judge learning? Standards identify the goals of learning.

Basically, two kinds of standards have been established in states and districts. On the one hand, content standards are those that define what students should know and be able to do. On the other hand, performance or achievement standards describe to what extent or degree of proficiency students must demonstrate. In other words, how good is good enough? Each state has the responsibility of answering that question relative to the content standards that it has developed. Although states have relatively established content standards, recent activity has come about in the area of performance standards in part due to the rigor of No Child Left Behind (NCLB). Prior to NCLB, some states had set rigorous performance standards only to realize that under NCLB this same initial rigor would in the end penalize them under the new adequate yearly progress (AYP) conditions.

States have developed performance descriptors or performance rubrics to serve as the measure of what students need to demonstrate to show various levels of proficiency. Here is an example of a performance rubric with descriptors for partially proficient, proficient, and advanced. Each performance descriptor defines what and how students must demonstrate a skill in order to obtain a score within a specific level (refer to Box 2.1).

CHANGING OF THE TIDE

In the midst of this process is the strong undercurrent (or, should we say, riptide) of how schools will be held accountable for the integrity and implementation of standards. To make any sense of the standards-based movement, there must be an accountability plan that addresses instruction, assessment, and intervention for those students who are not yet proficient. Without a comprehensive accountability plan or road map that addresses all components of student achievement, including support and leadership from the top, the current reform movement will be seen as another bandwagon that made its way through town. It, too, shall pass.

WHERE IS LAKE WOBEGON, ANYWAY?

Like it or not, all schools must be accountable for their students' performance. No matter how large or small or on what side of town the schools are located, we must continually ask ourselves, "Are students learning what they should? How do we know that schools are making progress in educating all students? What are we doing to support schools that are not making progress?" Because no one has ever been able to locate the community of Lake Wobegon, where "all the children are above average," the need to take a close look at standards and assessments that include all students continues to be central to reform today.

There are some basic principles that we need to be sure are in place to ensure that standards-based reform and accountability have a solid foundation on which to build. Examine the following principles, and see which ones you have in place in your school, district, or state:

Box 2.1

Examples of Content and Performance Standards

Reading

Content Standard 5: Students will read to locate, select, and make use of relevant information from a variety of media, reference, and technological sources.

Performance Descriptors for Grades K–4

Partially Proficient: Students inconsistently find and make use of information by using organization features of a variety of printed texts and electronic media. Students take notes and outline and identify main ideas in resource material, but there might be inaccuracies, limited understanding, omission of important facts and details, or direct copying.

 Proficient: Students are able to find and make use of information by using organizational features of a variety of printed texts and electronic media for a specific topic or purpose. Students accurately take notes, outline and identify main ideas in resource materials, and give credit by listing sources.

 Advanced: Students can easily and without assistance find information by using organization features of a variety of printed texts and electronic media. Students sort, record, and synthesize information from a wide variety of sources and give credit by listing sources.

Mathematics

Content Standard 6: Students link concepts and procedures as they develop and use computational techniques, including estimation, mental arithmetic, the paper-and-pencil method, calculators, and computers in problem-solving situations and communicate the reasoning that is used in solving these problems.

Performance Descriptors for Grades 9–12

Partially Proficient: With some procedural errors, students uses ratios, proportions, and percents in problem-solving situations. Students use a limited range of methods for computing with real numbers, selecting from among mental arithmetic, estimation, the paper-and-pencil method, calculator and computer methods and they make an attempt to determine whether the results are reasonable. Students describe some limitations of estimation, and incompletely assess the amount of error resulting from estimation.

 Proficient: In problem-solving situations, students use ratios, proportions, and percents. Students select and use appropriate methods for computing with real numbers. Students select from among mental arithmetic, estimation, the paper-and-pencil method, calculator and computer methods and determine whether the results are reasonable. Students describe the limitations of estimation and assess the amount of error resulting from estimation within acceptable limits.

(Continued)

(Continued)

Advanced: In problem-solving situations, students use ratios, proportions, and percents. Students select and use appropriate methods for computing with real numbers. Students select from mental arithmetic, estimation, the paper-and-pencil method, calculator and computer methods and provide insightful arguments that the results are reasonable. Students thoroughly describe the limitations of estimation and assess the amount of error resulting from estimation within acceptable limits.

SOURCE: Reprinted with permission from Hansche, L. (1998). *Meeting the requirements of Title I: Handbook for the development of performance standards.* Washington, DC: United States Department of Education.

- *The accountability system is accountable to itself.* By this we mean, who is monitoring the integrity of the current accountability system? How do we know it is doing what it is supposed to? How do we ensure that the highest level of ethical practices is taking place? And how do we make certain that practices are being consistently implemented and reported consistently across schools, districts, and states?

- *Accountability is built on standards that reflect all students in our schools.* This requires an examination of what is really going on at school sites across districts. Even though we know that standards in many places were developed without students with disabilities or second language learners in mind, these same students must now meet the same proficiency standards as all other students for whom the standards were originally written. With that in mind, it is critical that school leaders examine what is needed to support teachers to reach those standards with all students. In some states, standards are being reevaluated, extended, or expanded to encompass a greater community of students.

- *The opportunity to learn is a primary element in the accountability system.* That is, are all students, including students with disabilities and English language learners (ELLs), being given the opportunity to learn the standards? If not, why not? What needs to be done to make this happen? With the onslaught of more states mandating high-stakes exit exams to graduate (24 states at the printing of this book), not to mention lawsuits over them, it is imperative to make sure that all students are given the opportunity to learn what they need to know to have equal access to information needed to pass these exams.

- *All constituents of the accountability system have a clear understanding of the components of the accountability system, including any rewards and/or sanctions.* Do all members of your teaching community, including parents, administrators, and students, have a clear understanding of what the accountability system really is? If you don't explain it to them and check for understanding, the media will. Proactive communication about what is expected of all of those impacted by the system is critical for garnering support to make and support change.

Trademarks of a Standards-Based Classroom

Standards-based instruction, standards-based classrooms, or standards-based anything nicely rolls off the tongue. But what does it really look like in the classroom? What are the trademarks of a successful standards-based classroom? Try the following concepts on for size:

Students know the standards and level of proficiency required. Effective educators announce up front the standards, goals, and proficiency requirements—at the start of each semester, unit of lesson, and instruction—and they reinforce these requirements throughout instruction. They see instruction and assessment as inextricably linked. Nothing is kept secret. In fact, students are part of some of the instructional planning. After all, it is proficiency—not seat time—that matters in standards-based classrooms.

Students are provided multiple opportunities to learn. Students are given opportunities to revise, review, and debate their work over the course of days or during a unit of instruction. Unfortunately, this method is not widely used. Often, students are given one chance to get it right. We all know of teachers who give assignments and never return them or give students a grade without corrective feedback or the opportunity to revise. Whatever happened to mastery learning?

Student assignments reflect an integration of facts, concepts, and strategies. Assignments reflect the depth and breadth of skills that are being taught. They do not simply skim the surface. Students are given the opportunity, over the period of several days or during an even more extended period of time, to integrate their knowledge of a topic with other academic areas. In a standards-based classroom, teachers are aware of the standards in other content areas and integrate and reinforce them wherever and whenever possible.

Each assignment is an assessment in itself. Teachers in standards-based classrooms understand that instruction and assessment are an inextricably linked cycle. Instruction feeds assessment, and vice versa. There is no such thing as busywork. Each assignment or activity serves a purpose—to provide guided or independent practice and to assess learning.

Aligning IEPs With Standards

Among the many changes in special education law is the restructuring of the IEP to include (1) what assessment that students who have disabilities will participate in, and (2) what accommodations are needed. Before the changes in law, the IEPs of most students who have disabilities have reflected only individualized goals and objectives, without linking them to anything even remotely related to the general education curriculum. There are a variety of reasons why this situation might have been true:

- Lack of general expectations for students who have disabilities to achieve the general education curriculum
- Lack of professional development for administrators and general and special educators

- Lack of collaboration between special educators and general educators in general education reforms
- Lack of visionary leadership
- TTWWADI (pronounced ta-waa-di), or "That's the way we've always done it."

The bottom line is that we know more today than ever before about what works in learning, instruction, and assessment. The tragedy is that we do not always show what we know.

Linking the IEP to Standards

Today, more and more states are beginning to move in the direction of recommending one format for all IEPs. Past practice has been to list all required components of the IEP and to provide an example or model IEP. In many districts, IEPs have been redeveloped to guide teachers through an errorless method of linking a goal to a state or district content standard. For example, the teacher identifies the goal (and objective for the students with significant cognitive disabilities), then indicates what content standard it addresses.

If you are in a state that has established a set of broad standards (let's say eight) for students who have significant cognitive disabilities, then you would perhaps have at least eight IEP goals and objectives reflecting instruction in these required areas. Some argue that this method takes the "I," or individualization, out of the IEP. But that is not the case. In addition to these areas, a student's IEP must reflect his or her current levels of need in the areas that might not be covered by standards. In this manner, a student's IEP reflects the standards being worked toward by other students, as well as individual areas that are in need of further development. Box 2.2 has an example of a standards-based IEP. The goals and objectives reflect the district standards for all students. Each objective is linked to a standard or area in the general curriculum.

Unpacking Standards Once we have the IEP goals linked to the standards, then what? How do we *teach* the standards? What do the standards look like in the instructional process? How do we know that we have taught to the standard? All of these questions are critical in the process of aligning standards, instruction, and assessment.

The terms *backmapping and unpacking standards* are relatively new. These terms have evolved from the need to link standards to instruction in order to align the instruction with assessment. Once you have identified the desired result of learning (standards and benchmarks), you can then begin the instructional process by asking assessment questions.

- How will I know my students have an in-depth understanding of what I have taught?
- What will the evidence be?
- What assessment tasks will enable me to determine the extent to which students have learned the content?
- How can I use these assessment tasks to anchor my unit of instruction, lessons, and assignments?

Box 2.2

Individualized Education Program (IEP) Format Linking District Standards and Student Annual Goals for Students With Significant Cognitive Disabilities

Example 1

Student: Yu Kanduit DOB: 10/24/93

Content Area: Language Arts   **District Standard Area:** Participating in Discussion

District Standard: Students will engage productively in discussions to clarify thoughts; to explore issues, feelings, and experiences; to extend understanding; and to interact effectively with others.

Annual Goal: Yu Kanduit will use the Picture Exchange Communication System (PECS) to indicate wants and needs with 70% accuracy.

Objective 1: Yu will use PECS to indicate the need for water and/or the restroom with 70% accuracy by December 2005.

Objective 2: Yu will use PECS to request an activity of his choice with 100% accuracy by February 2006.

Objective 3: Yu will count the number of girls and the number of boys in the class and draw a bar graph with 100% accuracy.

Objective 4: Yu will draw a bar graph that depicts his physical education class, including the numbers of boys, girls, and all students with 90% accuracy by January 2006.

Example 2

Student: Ima Gonatry DOB: 8/29/85

Content Area: Mathematics   **District Standard Area:** Discrete Mathematics

District Standard: Students will solve problems in the areas of counting, identifying the problem to be solved, and finding the best solutions.

Annual Goal 1: Ima Gonatry will create her personal daily schedule by using 24-hour and standard time.

Objective 1: Ima will write out her morning routine/schedule with 100% accuracy by September 20, 2005.

Objective 2: Ima will write out to the minute, using standard time, her morning schedule with 80% accuracy by October 31, 2005.

Annual Goal 2: Using counting techniques, Ima will chart and graph the results to various mathematic problems with 80% accuracy.

Objective 1: Ima will count the total number of students in the class and draw a bar graph of the results with 80% accuracy.

Objective 2: Ima will count the number of girls and the number of boys in the class and draw a bar graph with 100% accuracy.

Objective 3: Ima will draw a bar graph that depicts her physical education class, including the numbers of boys, girls, and all students with 90% accuracy by January 2006.

> **Box 2.3**
>
> **Steps for Unpacking Standards**
>
> 1. Select a standard.
>
> 2. Identify the level of the Bloom's Taxonomy for the standard.
>
> 3. Identify the concept, including prerequisite skills that are encompassed in this standard.
>
> 4. Identify the vocabulary that is encompassed in this standard.
>
> 5. Identify the critical attributes of the assessment that will directly assess this standard.
>
> 6. Identify sample open-ended/constructed response assessment questions.
>
> 7. Identify multiple choice stem assessment items.
>
> 8. Map out the unit of instruction and corresponding lessons that will allow you to teach all the concepts, prerequisites, and vocabulary you have identified.

The key is to explore the answers to each of these questions during the planning stage, before the start of instruction. Looking for the extent to which students can explain, interpret, apply, and give perspectives is a good place to start.

Here is how backmapping or the unpacking of standards works. Start with a standard—any standard. Examine the standard in terms of its elements of instruction. For example, let us examine the following reading standard:

Content Standard: Reading

Compare and contrast an original text to a summary to determine whether the summary accurately captures the main idea(s) and critical details and conveys the underlying meaning.

It is easy to see that this one standard contains several concepts, vocabulary, and prerequisite skills. In other words, there are many skills packed into one standard. Our job is now to unpack it and ferret out the necessary facts, concepts, and strategies, as well as prerequisite skills that will need to be taught to ensure students attain mastery of this standard (Box 2.3). For example, how do we know students have the prior knowledge needed to launch into this standard? Well, we don't, unless we preassess them on the specifically identified skills that are needed to learn and demonstrate mastery of the standard. Once all the concepts, vocabulary, and levels of cognition are identified, we can begin to create the blueprint for instruction. Oh, yeah . . . the levels of cognition are the good ol' Bloom's Taxonomy. Remember Benjamin Bloom (may he rest in peace) and his levels of cognition (Box 2.4)? You should find this book and dust it off! Good things die hard or not at all. Bloom's Taxonomy is back with a vengeance! Bloom's Taxonomy is the tool that helps us look into the breadth and depth of knowledge or level of thinking that is required of students in learning standards. It is critical to identify the level of cognition and then match your instruction to this level. In addition, Bloom's Taxonomy helps with developing instructional activities and corresponding assessments that reflect exactly what was taught or intended to be taught. This process has been around for a long, long time, but it has been too often forgotten or misplaced (maybe in Lake Wobegon?).

In Box 2.5, we unpack the previous reading standard for you. After completing this exercise, you will be ready to map out your unit or lesson of instruction that will encompass all the critical skills and vocabulary you need to teach. Then you can ease into creating formative and summative assessments, aligned with instruction, that will allow you to gather the data necessary to judge whether students have in fact learned what you intended them to via this standard.

Box 2.4

Bloom's Taxonomy

KNOWLEDGE: Rote recall of specific information, such as facts, terminology, and procedures

Example: What is the name of the assessment required by the state?

COMPREHENSION: Understanding of material, ability to translate, paraphrase, interpret, or extrapolate information

Example: What concept and strategies do the reading subtest measure?

APPLICATION: Ability to transfer information to new situations or settings

Example: Using the provided student test protocol, where has the student performed the best?

ANALYSIS: Ability to find the parts to a whole, finding the interconnectedness or relationship among parts

Example: How does effective instruction improve student performance?

SYNTHESIS: Structuring, organizing, or assembling parts into a logical whole (or vice versa)

Example: Can you propose a plan for improving student performance on assessments for your school?

EVALUATION: Ability to make judgments about the value, usefulness, and/or utility of materials or ideas, according to certain criteria

Example: Based on your plan, how will you know whether it accomplished the goal of improving student performance on assessments?

Box 2.5

The Outline/Shell for Unpacking Standards

Content Standard:

Bloom's Level for Standard:

Teaching Points	
Concepts	*Vocabulary*
Critical Attributes of Assessment:	
Sample Open-Ended or Constructed Response:	
Sample Multiple-Choice Stems:	

Example:

Content Standard: Reading 2.4

Compare and contrast the original text to a summary to determine whether the summary accurately captures the main idea(s) and critical details and conveys the underlying meaning.

Bloom's Level for Standard: Analysis & Evaluation

Teaching Points	
Concepts	*Vocabulary*
– main idea	– compare
– summary	– contrast
– critical details/noncritical details	– determine
– underlying meaning	– justify
– compare & contrast	– convey
– nonfiction text supports	– critical
– expository → essay, text supports	– summary
– graphic organizers	
– how text is organized	
– influence: implicit, explicit	

Critical Attributes of Assessment:

- nonfiction text
- summary of a text—teacher or student made
- read text & summarize
- determine accuracy of main idea, details, and underlying meaning

Sample Open-Ended/Constructed Response:

- What is the summary missing?
- Rewrite the summary to match/highlight the original text.
- Using a Venn diagram, compare the summary with the original text.
- What are some inferences in the original text that are explicit in the summary?

Sample Multiple-Choice Stems

Provide a summary passage for students and create multiple-choice stems that accompany each summary provided. Examples of multiple-choice stems that could accompany selected summary passages are as follows:

Which of the following details would be appropriate for the summary above: (Provide at least four detail options for the student to pick from.)

Which of the following is the most appropriate main idea for the given summary below: (Provide at least four main ideas for the student to pick from.)

Choose the underlying meaning that best fits the summary provided: (Provide at least four options for the student to pick from.)

Supporting the Process. Leadership and support are critical to all aspects of accountability and educational reform. So it goes with keeping the momentum of unpacking standards. In Box 2.6, we highlight several ways administration and teachers can work together to support the process of backmapping or unpacking standards. Because most schools have departments and department leaders (or grade-level leaders), we suggest some activities. A *walkthrough* is just that. Administrators and teacher leaders who walk through classes are looking and listening for evidence of standards-based instruction. Walkthroughs are *not* evaluative in nature. Rather, they are exploratory. Finally, the last section is really about the metacognitive processes that one goes through to decide which standard and why, which objective and why, and the necessary communication and corrective feedback important to the entire process of unpacking standards. Have fun!

SUMMARY

In this chapter, we discussed the trademarks of standards-based instruction. We examined the importance of incorporating standards into the IEP and showed a process for unpacking or backmapping them into instruction.

Box 2.6

Unpacking the Standards: Supporting the Process

Focus Question: How can principals provide leadership in helping teachers help students meet the standards?

Teacher/Department Collaboration

- Work with the department chair to schedule meeting time to discuss or unpack a standard.
- Departments collect data about how they teach and assess a given standard or cluster of standards and discuss the results with an eye toward developing an action plan to address gaps.
- Departments select a set of focus standards for unpacking, discussing, and collecting data on the standards for one year.
- Departments look at published test specs on state or district assessments to understand the standards and how they are assessed.

Walkthroughs

- Look for objectives aligned with the standard(s). (Caveat: Teachers may be working on a teaching point that is a prerequisite to the standard.)
- Look for proving behaviors aligned with the objective and the standard.
- Look at student work:
  - Are the assignments and assessments aligned with the standard(s)?
  - Are the tasks rigorous and appropriate for the grade level?
  - What types of feedback do you notice on student work?
  - How are the assignments scored or graded (rubrics, checklists, or letter grades)?
  - How often do students engage in real-world assessment tasks?
- Interview students: What are you learning or have you learned about standard X? What happens to your work once it has been corrected? How do you know when you have mastered one of the content standards? How do you know when your work isn't good enough? What opportunities do you have to improve your work when it isn't good enough?

Discussion With Teachers

- Which standard are you working on?
- How did you come to choose that standard(s)?
- What is your objective? How do you come to choose this objective?
- What came before this objective? What will come next?
- How do you plan to assess this standard?
- How do you differentiate your assessments to allow for multiple ways of demonstrating mastery of a standard?
- How do you communicate good enough to students?
- How do you provide opportunities for students to revise their work when it isn't good enough?
- How do students in your class know when their work isn't good enough?

Critical to the discussion of improving student performance is the need to align instruction with assessment. We reviewed Bloom's Taxonomy and the need to align the cognitive demands of how you teach with how you test. Finally, we raised issues and concerns about accountability for all students. Instruction matters. Accountability requires a top-down, bottom-up collaborative approach with a clear plan to support all in the process.

TEST YOUR KNOWLEDGE

In keeping with standards-based instruction, see how well you have learned the facts, concepts, and strategies presented in this chapter.

1. Standards provide a common _____ of student learning.

2. Achievement standards tell us how _____ is _____ enough.

3. A comprehensive accountability _____ or road map is necessary to facilitate successful standards base reform.

4. Proactive _____ about what is expected of all those impacted by the accountability system is critical for garnering support for change.

5. In standards-based classrooms, each assignment is an _____ in itself.

6. More and more states and districts have developed IEP forms that link goals and objectives to the _____ standard.

7. TTWWADI is the saying _____ _____ _____ _____ _____ _____ _____. This statement can be viewed as one of the reasons for the lack of progress in the fields of general and special education.

8. The process of backmapping is a way to _____ standards to instruction.

9. Backmapping or unpacking standards better assures that instruction and assessment are _____.

10. A walkthrough of classes is used to look and listen for _____ of standards-based instruction.

ANSWERS

1. measure (p. 13)
2. good, good (p. 14)
3. plan (old p. 14)
4. communication (p. 16)
5. assessment (p. 17)
6. That's the way we've always done it (p. 18)

7. content (p. 18)

8. link or connect (p. 18)

9. aligned (p. 18)

10. evidence (p. 23)

REFLECTIONS ON CHANGE

See Appendix A for the Reflections on Change activity for this chapter (p. 189).

RECOMMENDED RESOURCES

Bloom, B. (1956). *Taxonomy of educational objectives: The classification of educational goals: Handbook 1. Cognitive domain.* New York: McKay.

Courtade-Little, G., & Browder, D. W. (2005). *Aligning IEPs to academic standards.* Verona, WI: Attainment Co.

Elliott, J. L., & Thurlow, M. L. (1997). *Opening the door to educational reform: Understanding standards.* Boston: Federation for Children with Special Needs, Parents Engaged in Educational Reform (PEER) Project.

Linn, R. L. (1999). *Standards-based accountability: Ten suggestions.* Los Angeles: National Center for Research on Evaluation, Standards, and Student Testing.

Quality counts 2004: Count me in. Special education in an era of standards. (2004, January 8). [Special issue]. *Education Week, 23.*

Reeves, D. B. (1998). *Making standards work: How to implement standards-based assessments in the classroom, school and district.* Denver, CO: Center for Performance Assessment.

INTERNET RESOURCES

American Federation of Teachers: www.aft.org

Council of Chief State School Offices: www.ccsso.org

Education Commission of the States: www.ecs.org

Federation for Children with Special Needs: www.fcsn.org

Mid-Continent Research for Education and Learning (MCREL): www.mcrel.org

National Center on Educational Outcomes: www.nceo.info

National Center on Education and the Economy (NCEE): www.ncee.org

National Education Association: www.nea.org

Using Data to Drive Instruction

3

Data is not information any more than 50 tons of cement is a skyscraper.

—*Clifford Stoll*

Even if you are on the right track, you will get run over if you stay in the same place.

—*Anonymous*

Hot-Button Issues

- Those special education kids can't learn this content.
- The students with disabilities are going to keep us from making our adequate yearly progress (AYP)!
- We need to be sure to watch the special education numbers so we don't create another subgroup at the sites.

OPPORTUNITIES AND CHALLENGES

The No Child Left Behind (NCLB) Act has brought with it sweeping changes that many school districts and states are struggling to implement. With the theme of accountability for the achievement of all students, including students with disabilities, NCLB provides a rare and exciting opportunity for the field of special education. Think about it—this is the first time that accountability for students with disabilities has come from the general education side of the house. And, with it, lots of shifting in many proverbial accountability seats—sometimes uncomfortably. On the special education side of the house, however, for just as many years, folks have been asking for this comprehensive inclusion in accountability and assessment . . . and now it is here! But many special education administrators and personnel are incredibly concerned, even stressed about this "opportunity." The bottom line is that it has been ready, set, include—all in AYP. The overall concern with this approach is that we as an educational community have had a segregated approach to educating students with disabilities and now all students, including students with disabilities, are being held accountable to the same content standards. Great, great! But scary, scary! In fact, so scary that districts have started to look for loopholes. One of the unanticipated outcomes of any mandate is, unfortunately, that many will seek ways around them.

At every reauthorization of the Individuals With Disabilities Education Act (IDEA), there are and always have been changes and challenges for implementation. Let's face it—we as a nation have not yet fully implemented the new regulations of the last reauthorization of IDEA! Inclusive accountability and assessment for students with disabilities was a significant focus of the 1997 reauthorization. And even back then, many folks did not embrace the notion of accountability and assessment for students with disabilities. Folks certainly did not embrace the regulation of reporting the test performance of students with disabilities. So even as the Individuals With Disabilities Education Improvement Act of 2004 (IDEA 2004) begins its tenure, there is still much work to be done about the challenge of closing the achievement gap and improving assessment and accountability for students with disabilities.

Although we know that federal laws are mandated and regulated from Washington, DC, the spirit and integrity of the implementation of any law start in our own backyard. In the early days of state assessment reporting on students with disabilities, it was often the case that participation rates were the only thing reported. This has changed. Now both participation numbers and performance results of students with disabilities are required, as well as their access to general education content and curricula. A distinguished educator, Deborah McDonald, wrote it best when she penned, "By analyzing what is and what is not working to improve student learning, educators can focus scarce resources on goals and strategies that make the most impact on achievement. Time is the most critical resource. . . . The time invested in 'data work' can generate a net savings if it guides the school toward decisions that pay dividends in student achievement" (Holcomb, 1999, p. xiii). Because this book is about ways to improve student achievement and making the instruction–assessment connection, let's focus in on classroom, school, and district use of data.

Basic Data to Know

There are so many ways to sort and analyze data. However, our approach here will be simple, and you get to choose which data elements you want to know more about, already know, or can look at differently. Regardless of your role—principal, teacher, paraeducator, parent, board member, or superintendent, knowledge about these basic data elements is a must.

Demographics. In this day and age of subgroup performance, it is imperative to know your student demographics. How many and what types of students attend your district, school, or class? Things such as race, ethnicity, gender, poverty level, English language learners (ELLs) and those ELLs who have been redesignated as English proficient, and those eligible for free and reduced-price lunch are all common demographic variables to collect. Equally interesting is to analyze the demographics of your teaching staff in relation to student demographics. Sometimes the comparison of student and teacher demographics makes for interesting cause–effect interactions. When it comes to students with disabilities, you will want to know how many and what types or categories of students attend your district, school, or class (e.g., how many students with learning disabilities vs. mental retardation vs. speech only, male vs. female, etc.). And you will want to know what level of services students are receiving. Are more served in a self-contained classroom or in the general education setting? You can look closely at the types of students in the federal categories of disabilities. For example, how many ELLs are in the learning disability or mental retardation category? How many African American boys are categorized as having emotional disabilities? And who exactly makes up all the students with speech impairments? Are there patterns?

These data are important because as you begin to look at test scores and other performance indicators, you will be able to generate hypotheses as well as set targets to address or remediate them. For example, you may find that resource room students outperform general education students, or students with emotional disabilities in self-contained placements outperform the students in resource rooms. And you may even find that all of these students outperformed the general education students! One just never knows until the data are disaggregated.

Of course, you will want to know similar demographics about the general student population as well. This is very important because you should refrain from making decisions based on one data set. Whenever looking at special education student performance data, we highly recommend that you compare these data to data from the general education cohort peers, even by gender, to see whether there is a comparable trend.

Achievement Data. How many times have you heard "Those kids with disabilities are pulling down our test scores," or "Those disabled kids can't learn this content," or something like this? Have you ever stopped, wondered, and looked at data to see whether that, in fact, was true? And, if it is true, what are we as a staff or an educational community doing about it? Although in some cases you may find that some students with disabilities may underperform—what are we actually doing to address it in the classroom? Who is monitoring what goes on in the classroom, and what standards students are being taught? Depending on the grade level you are interested in, looking at academic grades is a fun place to start. Let's look at high school students for this example. A fun little activity is to obtain a printout of all students who have Individualized Education Programs (IEPs) in your school. Once obtained, look at the students receiving resource services. How are they doing in their core content classes? Their special education support classes? Then get a printout of the general education students and make a cross-comparison of grades between these groups. Are the special education students really doing more poorly than the general education students, somewhat poorly, or about the same?

The Long Beach Unified School District did these kinds of data examinations and found that 50–70% of all high school students receiving resource services had multiple D's and F's on their report cards. This apparently had been going on for years. Then staff looked at the type of resource service delivery that was being used—collaborative or coteaching versus pullout. (*Pullout* is defined here as students pulled out of their general education classrooms and into special education classes for core content instruction for math, English, etc.) Guess what they found? Coteaching in these high schools simply didn't work. Guess what else they found? The pullout model wasn't that much better. So, is this about the student, the teaching model, the lack of access to standards, poor instruction, or all of the above? You can't answer that question until the data are disaggregated and analyzed. Closer analysis also revealed that some of the students were getting great grades in the resource classroom but failing in their other content courses. Hmmm.

Based on these data, the district went about the business of changing how students received resource support and where core content instruction was delivered. The high schools instituted a study skills curriculum, Strategies for Success (SFS), coupled with core academic support (see Box 3.1 for an overview of the course). For a complete review of course outlines by grade level, see Internet Resources at end of this chapter. The results after one year of implementation were astonishing: D's and F's went down while C's, B's, and A's went up (see Box 3.2)!

So, for this district, data-based decision making proved very fruitful in making systemic changes for the betterment of student learning. Keep in mind that other districts may take different approaches; what works for one district may not be a good match for another district. In this example, data revealed that collaboration or coteaching was not a good match! The critical piece is that data are part of determining whether a change in approaches, methodologies, and/or programs are doing what they are expected to do—make student learning happen.

Once these data were discovered and the benefits of the program change to students were assessed, the district looked at middle school test scores and grades across both content and resource classes. It so happened that the district was in the midst of testing eighth graders, using multiple measures, to place them in the high school reading intervention programs at the high school. What they found was that many of the resource students performed below proficient on the state assessments, both norm-referenced and standards-based, in the area of English language arts. And they scored 1–3 out of 50 on a basic reading placement test—putting them at the *pop, top, mop* reading skill level. It is interesting to note that these same students were receiving A's in their resource pullout English language arts classes. Sadly, these students were being set up for failure in the high schools they were about to enter. Of course, their impact on overall site test results would be less favorable as well. So how exactly do these interesting findings manifest themselves? And if they hadn't been discovered, would more of the same for these students be continued, thereby continuing the failure cycle for these kids? And the familiar spin of "those kids with disabilities are pulling our scores down" could have, in fact, been very much

Box 3.1

Strategies for Success (SFS) Overview (Excerpt From LBUSD's SFS Program)

High School

Given the current Resource Specialist Program (RSP) model in the high schools, 50–70% of the RSP students are failing. The current model is collaborative, and students do not receive one-on-one support from their RSP teacher. Instead, RSP teachers float into classes to check on students. No direct instruction occurs.

This year, the district revamped the entire RSP program at all the high schools. The impetus for this was an overwhelming failure rate, the California High School Exit Exam (CAHSEE), and the No Child Left Behind (NCLB) Act.

The current high school model is a new course called Strategies for Success (SFS). This is a credit-bearing course in which students are scheduled in a pullout model to receive small group and one-to-one instruction with their RSP teacher. During the first half of the session, students are instructed in skills they need to be successful in their core content classes (e.g., note taking, study skills, notebook organization, time management, etc.). The second half of the class is spent preteaching, previewing, or reviewing core content material students are learning.

I. Course Description

This course is designed for students in RSP, Grades 6–12. The students enrolled in this course are identified as needing RSP support in a variety of skill and academic areas. For students to benefit from classroom teaching, they must exhibit certain appropriate and effective learning and school behaviors. When students exhibit these behaviors, a better teaching and learning environment is the result. The curriculum contains a scope and sequence to address different areas of support at each grade level.

First part of the period or block:

Teachers are to use the Long Beach Unified School District (LBUSD) Curriculum Map and Curriculum Guide to teach appropriate learning and school behaviors, such as organizational skills and study skills. Direct instruction and essential elements of effective instruction lesson delivery are crucial.

Various components of direct instruction include continuous communication of expectations, instructional objective and targeted instruction of a behavior or strategy, modeling, guided practice, checking for understanding, independent practice, and feedback. Instruction should include extension or immediate application of skills to learning activities or assignments.

Second half of the period or block:

In addition to daily direct study skills instruction, this course will apply various learning strategies that students should use to complete assignments in academic classes. Students receive additional pullout support for their academic classes by having an RSP teacher preteach, reteach, and review concepts, and model and teach strategies that give students tools to access and successfully complete the work required of them in general education classes.

These strategies are designed to provide students with systematic procedures for completing common school tasks (i.e., projects, essays, daily assignments) to increase their academic success in general education classes. Teachers may continue to use site-based curriculum to provide consistency in the instruction that students receive.

(Continued)

(Continued)

This portion of the class should not be used as a study hall.

I. RSP Teacher's Role

The RSP teacher will no longer teach students in a collaborative model or in pullout math, English, or reading classes.

The RSP teacher will teach SFS, daily, to small groups of students. Some high schools may elect to have a couple of RSP teachers teach a reading intervention course, as well as SFS. Because there are fewer RSP teachers at middle school, all RSP teachers will teach SFS only.

The RSP teacher will continue to monitor IEP goals, as well as teach grade level SFS curriculum, support students in learning and completing content area material and assignments, conduct ongoing communication with the general education teachers, develop action plans for those students receiving D's or F's, and attend scheduled SFS workshops.

II. IEP Goals and Objectives

The IEP goals should be developed based on student instructional need, not on program or teacher. RSP teachers will *still* monitor IEP goals progress. However, if RSP goals are written that allude to RSP math or English, then goals must be rewritten to align with SFS and skills the student need to progress in his content area classes. Also, an IEP goal should be written, based on student need, in the area of study skills, organization, test preparation, completing assignments, and the like.

Sample goals and objectives for SFS can be found in each curriculum guide.

III. Communication With General Education Teachers

1. Probably the most important first step is to verbally, and face to face, personally communicate with the school staff what SFS is through department meetings, staff meetings, conference period meetings, and so forth. It is important to answer the teachers' obvious question "What's in it for me?" by talking about the benefits of SFS for them as general education teachers (e.g., support from another teacher to teach—discrete skills needed for an assignment, completion of homework, test taking, use of accommodations—and/or to collaborate with to strategize and develop a plan for specific students). RSP teachers must develop a plan to communicate with the general education teachers regarding student assignments, homework assignments, completion of assignments, upcoming tests, test scores or retakes, behavior, attendance, and the like.

2. The curriculum includes a biweekly General Education Teacher Report that each RSP student gives to his or her general education teacher to complete. This report gives the RSP student and teacher a marker of the student's current grade, homework completion, and attendance for each class the student is enrolled in. This report is part of the student's SFS grade.

3. In addition to the biweekly report, RSP teachers often e-mail or put notes in their general education teachers' mailboxes regarding weekly homework assignments, upcoming tests, and so forth. RSP teachers must initiate and continuously prompt and reinforce general educators to participate in this communication.

4. Plan open houses for staff and reinforce and recognize teachers for returning the biweekly report or homework requests. For example, tell the administrator who is supporting the SFS model with great communication or other methods.

Box 3.2

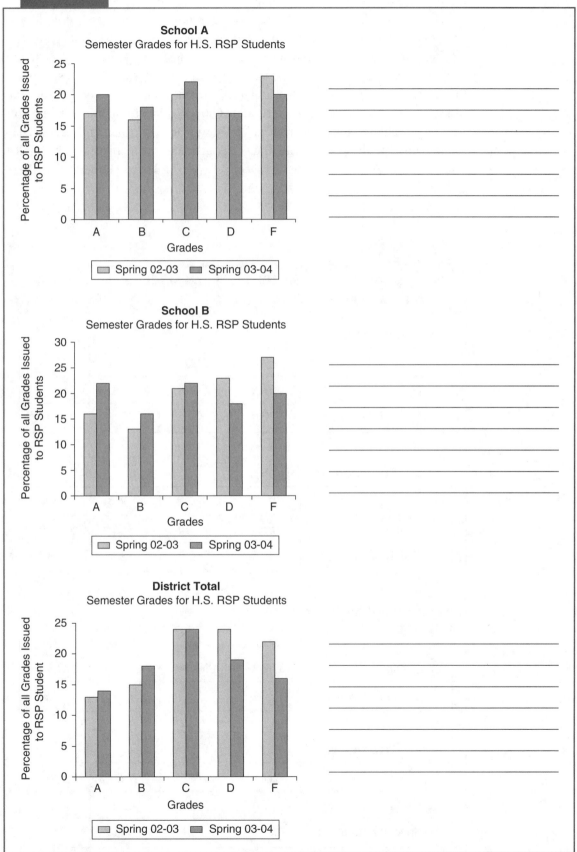

reality. Again, based on this discovery through the use of data, instructional models and the content of that instruction were changed dramatically.

Our final example includes the disaggregation of achievement data of students with disabilities based on a principal's comment, "My special education teachers are the best. They work so hard and push our kids to high learning standards and expectations. Yet, the kids don't show it on their test scores." Based on this comment, the district administrator took a hard look at the state test score data for this principal's students with disabilities and immediately notified the principal to start celebrating. The hard work was paying off as shown by the overall growth of 38 points and 57 points these students made in English language arts and mathematics, respectively (Box 3.3). And it didn't stop there.

Box 3.3

Comparison of 2003 and 2004 ELA and Math for Special Education Students

District Summary

	2003	2003	2004	2004
Group	ELA	Math	ELA	Math
Special Education	339	328	371	370

School A (Elementary School)

	2003	2003	2004	2004
Group	ELA	Math	ELA	Math
Special Education	385	443	423	500

School B (Middle School)

	2003	2003	2004	2004
Group	ELA	Math	ELA	Math
Special Education	341	361	487	519

School C (High School)

	2003	2003	2004	2004
Group	ELA	Math	ELA	Math
Special Education	325	234	351	285

This same district administrator calculated and disaggregated the test score data of all students with disabilities for every school in the district. The results were overwhelmingly positive in growth!

Had not this data disaggregation been done, the district administrators from both the top down and the bottom up would have continued to make the unanchored observation that students with disabilities could not meet the same high standards or, in fact, could not learn at all!

Instructional Programs and Test Performance Data. How do we know whether the programs we are teaching are, in turn, giving us the results we desire on tests? More important, how do we know that students are learning and closing the gap between skill deficits and strengths? Here we want to look at all students, both general education and those receiving special education services, and their performance on, let's say, academic performance indicators. It doesn't matter whether the instructional program is homegrown or a published off-the-shelf program—we need to ask how students, including those with disabilities, are performing. One way to do this is to disaggregate data surrounding instructional programs by some overall indicator, such as the state test performance. We believe that many great things in education are stopped because of the lack of sufficient data or actual data analysis. However, insufficient or ineffective practices are continued because they are not examined closely. In this day and age of subgroups and test performance, closing the achievement gap and AYP, it makes total sense to examine and disaggregate data for instructional and achievement purposes—for all students, including students with disabilities.

In Box 3.4, you will find California's Academic Performance Index (API) comparison of reading programs that the Long Beach Unified School District had been implementing in its high schools. These achievement data were disaggregated to find out whether the high schools were in fact getting their bang for the buck, as the saying goes, for all the resources and training being poured into the implementation of these reading programs. District officials also wanted to know whether the reading programs that were teacher made (Literacy Workshop) were still worthy of use or should be set aside for the newer off-the-shelf published programs. You will note that the data were disaggregated by general education students, students with disabilities served in self-contained settings, and IEP/ELL students.

A perusal of the data shows that, in fact, the newly implemented literacy program, Language! I and II, was showing positive results. The Lindamood-Bell Phoneme Sequencing Program, although known for its relevance to elementary school students, was implemented in the high school with students who had similar literacy needs. After the second year of state assessment administration, it was clear that it was having an impact with students at the preliteracy skill level. To many people's surprise, the Literacy Workshop was showing incredible gains for the students enrolled in it. Through the analysis of data, the Literacy Workshop showed district personnel its worth and impact of student growth. It was a *keeper* program. Another result of this analysis is that the district decided to discontinue its use of SMART2Tel, a published reading program. Its cost did not equal its worth in student achievement.

Box 3.4

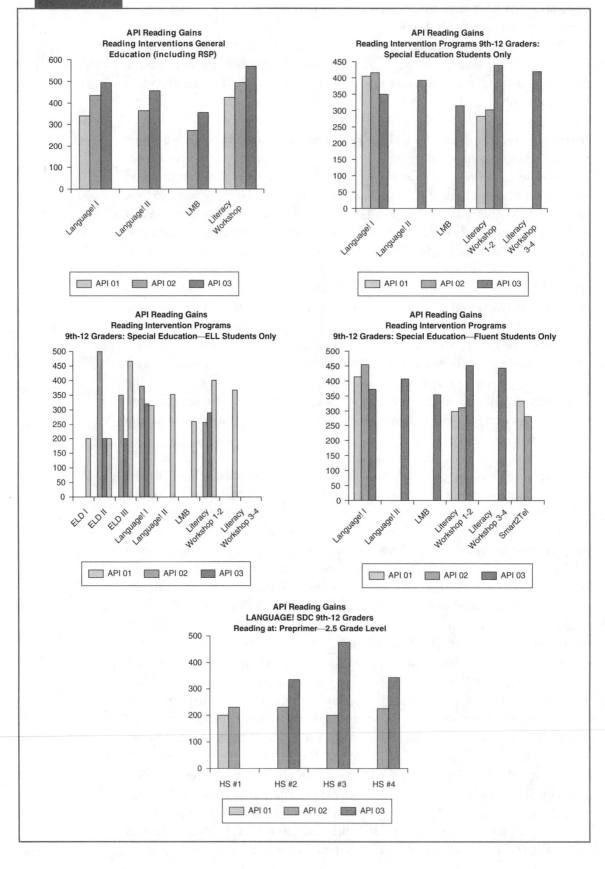

Finally, the district wanted to see how students with disabilities enrolled in self-contained special education classes were faring in the Language! I and II programs. These students were receiving this reading instruction from a Language!-trained special education teacher. The results of four high schools are shown. In fact, all students, including students with disabilities, were showing substantial growth in the reading program.

When all was said and done, the results of these analyses were shared with teaching staff. You can imagine the morale boost.

Working From Ground Zero. Another very familiar scenario surrounding instructional programs and test performance can be found in Box 3.5. This is a case study discussion worthy of review and thought. We often meet students like Paco, who, despite good attendance and command of the language, are not meeting with success in the day-to-day requirements of school. In this case, a review of data will need to include an assessment of requisite and prerequisite skills he may or may not have yet mastered to allow him success in passing the exams. It may be these very skills that are lacking that are precluding Paco from fully accessing the curriculum. In addition, we will want to inventory his test-taking skills (see Chapter 5 for more details). For Paco, it could be skill deficit, lack of test-taking strategies, or a combination of both. The only way to find this out is to generate hypotheses of what could be causing the failure, dig into the data to see what the exact cause or causes are, and then, of course, make a plan of action or intervention.

Box 3.5

Case Study Discussion

Directions: Use the following case study to discuss issues around creating and using data-based decision-making practices. Talk about what changes could be done to increase this student's performance in the classroom and other requirements.

You are a member of a grade-level team. Your student, Paco, a 10th grader, is currently receiving resource room services. He is bilingual and is proficient in English and the language spoken in the home. Paco has good attendance, works hard to complete assignments, and seeks extra help when needed, yet he struggles tremendously in school. In particular, he has difficulty in math and science. Paco is not a candidate for the alternate assessment. He takes the regular state and district assessments.

Your state mandates that all students must pass an end-of-course exam to get credit for courses enrolled in. Paco has failed both the 9th- and 10th-grade end-of-course exams in math and science. In fact, he was not successful in summer school either.

What can be done for Paco? What needs to be examined and changed? What is your plan of action to review existing data to begin to develop an instructional plan for Paco?

In this section, we gave you at least three different situations in which the need and exploration of data for specific areas of concern or interest have proven useful and prolific. Using data to drive instructional decisions is not difficult to do and is worth its weight in instructional gold!

QUESTIONS YOU SHOULD BE ASKING, AND ANSWERS YOU SHOULD KNOW

In this chapter, we worked to bring to light the importance of data to drive instruction and systemic change. Regardless of your position, you should be asking important and sometimes tough questions.

Principals/District Administrators

Work with your assessment office or research department to obtain disaggregated test performance on your students with disabilities every year. Be sure you have the general education data as well so that you can make a comparison. Although you may or may not have a significant subgroup of special education students at your site (depending on your state's identified subgroup size and size of your school), it is really important to know how all your special education students performed. Most test results will only give you the significant subgroup performance, leaving you with no idea how the students with disabilities performed.

Special education administrators and site principals also should examine patterns of use of accommodations. Previous data show a pattern of fewer accommodations being used in high schools than in middle schools than in elementary schools during state testing. This is a pattern that is contrary to what is probably best practice. The bigger question is—Why are students using accommodations less as they move up in grade levels? Perhaps they never really needed them? Or perhaps they do not want to use them for fear they would "stick out and look like a geek," as one student said. Without looking at the data, the pattern might go hidden.

An interesting little study to conduct is to randomly select some IEPs across all grade levels. Review the IEPs to see what accommodations were written in the document and then cross-reference them with those accommodations provided to that student during the district or state assessment. Do the study vice versa as well. See what accommodations were given on testing day and cross-reference them with what was actually written on the student's IEP. You may be amazed at what you find!

And, of course, we know there are policies in some states that currently penalize schools and/or students if students require the use of accommodations that are deemed nonstandard by the state. That is, if a student uses a needed but nonstandard accommodation, the student's score automatically falls into the "far below basic" level of proficiency. And this will happen regardless of how well the student does on the test. However, students should never be denied the use of these needed nonstandard accommodations just because of a state policy. It is the state policy that needs to be examined, not the needed use of the accommodation. In reality, it is these kinds of policies that put teachers, IEP teams, and administrators at odds when they try to determine how to do the right thing for students while increasing the performance data at the school site.

Other patterns also might exist that need to be questioned. For example, are students with emotional and behavioral disabilities not receiving accommodations during testing? Are students of certain ethnic backgrounds receiving proportionately fewer accommodations than students of other ethnic backgrounds? To obtain answers to these questions, certain data collection mechanisms need to be in place. However, with the enactment of IDEA 2004, which requires that states report on the number of students who were provided accommodations, these mechanisms are going to have to be developed and implemented.

Teachers

Be sure to get the data previously discussed. Don't take no for an answer. Get some sort of indication of how your students are doing and how they have done over the past three years, and get these data for both the general assessment and the alternate assessment.

Parents

Be sure you clearly understand your district and state's assessment and accountability systems. Look at the results that are reported to you and ask questions about them. Be sure to obtain the scores of your child, even if he or she is in a subgroup with numbers too small to be reported publicly.

Board Members

It is important that you thoroughly understand the ins and outs of your state's assessment system. These systems, the accountability indexes and AYP, are a wonderland of confusion. For you to make good policy decisions about instruction, materials, and funding, to name a few, it is important to know and understand subgroup performance, growth indexes, and the impact of test results on district accountability for NCLB.

Superintendents

You need to know everything already mentioned and more. You are the educational leader in your district, and you are a role model for expectations for learning and instruction. When discussion about subgroup performance comes up, or as you look at reasons for why some schools or even your district did not make AYP, it is imperative that high expectations for all students be communicated. Recently, we heard a superintendent indicate that the numbers of students with disabilities would be monitored at sites to be sure "another subgroup would not be created for school sites to deal with." Ouch! Why that subgroup? Why not another subgroup? And, more tragically, what message does that send to principals about accountability for all students? And, what about the teachers of students with disabilities who teach these students on a daily basis? This is definitely not a morale booster or one that embraces the philosophy *all means all*, or No Child Left Behind.

SUMMARY

In this chapter we discussed the many facets and uses of data to drive instruction as well as make instructional changes to improve student achievement. We emphasized the importance of context in analyzing data (e.g., demographics). Additionally, we made it clear that students with disabilities' data can be disaggregated and used for instruction or progress monitoring even though they may not be considered a significant subgroup in your state. Hence, most often in these cases, students' specific score results are not reported and often remain unknown to administrators and, more important, teachers who are working hard in the trenches. Data create power and fun all at the same time.

TEST YOUR KNOWLEDGE

1. Lots of folks are stressed about this new "opportunity" NCLB provides for all students, including _____ _____ _____.

2. The spirit and integrity of the implementation of any _____ starts in our own backyard.

3. Sometimes the comparison of student and teacher _____ makes for interesting cause–effect interactions.

4. One should refrain from making decisions based on _____ data set.

5. By examining achievement data you may find that "those kids with disabilities" are in fact not bringing _____ your test scores.

6. You may find by looking at grades across content areas that general education and special education students are not performing that _____.

7. It is imperative to analyze program data to see whether in fact the program is _____.

8. Sometimes in education we continue a program because we _____ it is working. But when we look at the data, we find that the program is_____.

9. It is important to disaggregate _____ for students with disabilities, even if they are not a significant subgroup in your state.

10. Disaggregating data for all students, including students with disabilities, allows us to be sure what we are doing is improving student _____.

ANSWERS

1. students with disabilities (p. 28)

2. law (p. 28)

3. demographics (p. 29)

4. one (p. 29)

5. down (p. 29)

6. differently (p. 29)

7. working or achieving results (p. 30)

8. think/not (p. 35)

9. data (p. 38)

10. achievement or results or performance (p. 40)

REFLECTIONS ON CHANGE

See Appendix A for the Reflections on Change activity for this chapter (p. 189).

RECOMMENDED RESOURCES

Bernhardt, V. L. (1998). *Data analysis for comprehensive schoolwide improvement.* Larchmont, NY: Eye On Education.

Elliott, J. (2003). Assessment and accountability for students with disabilities: Putting theory into practice. In J. E. W. Wall & G. R. Waltz (Eds.), *Measuring up: Assessment issues for teachers, counselors, and administrators* (pp. 177–196). Greensboro, NC: CAPS.

Elliott, J. (2003). Assessment, accommodations, and accountability: The good, the bad, and the ugly. *Urban Perspectives, 8*(1), 10–14.

Elliott, J., Thurlow, M., & Ysseldyke, J. (1996). *Assessment guidelines that maximize the participation of students with disabilities in large-scale assessments: Characteristics and considerations* (Synthesis Report 25). Minneapolis: University of Minnesota, National Center on Educational Outcomes.

Erickson, R., Ysseldyke, J., & Thurlow, M. (1996). *Neglected numerators, drifting denominators, and fractured fractions: Determining participation rates for students with disabilities in statewide assessment programs* (Synthesis Report 23). Minneapolis: University of Minnesota, National Center on Educational Outcomes.

Erickson, R., Ysseldyke, J., Thurlow, M., & Elliott, J. (1997). *Reporting the results of students with disabilities in state and district assessments* (NCEO Policy Directions 8). Minneapolis: University of Minnesota, National Center on Educational Outcomes.

Greene Fell, J. (2001). *Language!* Longmont, CO: Sopris West.

Holcomb, E. L. (1999). *Getting excited about data: How to combine people, passion, and proof.* Thousand Oaks, CA: Corwin.

Jaeger, R. M., & Tucker, C. G. (1998). *Analyzing, disaggregating, reporting, and interpreting students' achievement test results: A guide to practice for Title I and beyond.* Washington, DC: Council of Chief State School Officers.

Lindamood, P., & Lindamood, P. (1991). *Lindamood phoneme sequencing program.* San Luis Obispo, CA: Gander Educational.

McGrew, K. S., Thurlow, M. L., & Spiegel, A. (1993). An investigation of the exclusion of students with disabilities in national data collection programs. *Educational Evaluation and Policy Analysis, 15*(3), 339–352.

Quinn, D., Greunert, S., & Valentine, J. (1999). *Using data for school improvement.* Reston, VA: National Association of Secondary School Principals.

Steverson, M., & Steverson, R. [AU: Please provide date]. *SMART2Tel.* Marina Del Rey, CA: Learning Links.

Thurlow, M., Olsen, K., Elliott, J., Ysseldyke, J., Erickson, R., & Ahearn, E. (1996). *Alternate assessments for students with disabilities* (NCEO Policy Directions 5). Minneapolis: University of Minnesota, National Center on Educational Outcomes.

Thurlow, M., Scott, D., & Ysseldyke, J. (1995). *A compilation of states' guidelines for including students with disabilities in assessments* (Synthesis Report 17). Minneapolis: University of Minnesota, National Center on Educational Outcomes.

Ysseldyke, J., Thurlow, M., & Olsen, K. (1996). *Self-study guide for the development of statewide assessments that include students with disabilities.* Minneapolis: University of Minnesota, National Center on Educational Outcomes.

INTERNET RESOURCES

Education Trust: www.edtrust.org

Long Beach Unified School District: www.lbusd.k12.ca.us (Scroll to "Curriculum" for a complete review of Strategies for Success course outlines by grade level.)

1-3 Self-Check:

Where Do I Stand?

Evaluate and reflect on the following statements as a personal survey of where you stand in relation to the information presented thus far. Base your answers to these questions on the topics that are presented in this book and on what you think that you already know and are doing.

Self-Check for Chapter 1

- I have a good sense of what I have been emphasizing to increase the test performance of students and what I still really need to learn about to be more effective.

Self-Check for Chapter 2

- I now see the connection between the basic principles of an accountability system and the trademarks of a standards-based classroom.
- I understand the strategy of backmapping or unpacking standards. I see the importance of doing this and understand how it can help me teach, and my students learn, the skills they need to master content standards.

Self-Check for Chapter 3

- I know the basic demographic data about the students who attend my class, school, or district.
- I understand the value of disaggregating assessment results by students with and without disabilities and comparing the differences. This includes district and state assessment data as well as adequate yearly progress (AYP).
- I understand the importance of using the data from assessments to make important instruction decisions about whether what we are doing and how we are teaching students is working.

Making Sound Accommodations Decisions

Education is not preparation for life, it is life itself.

—*John Dewey*

He may read at the second grade level, but that doesn't mean he *thinks* at the second grade level.

—*Margaret McLaughlin*

Hot-Button Issues

- There is too much to do during instruction already. How can we be expected to provide accommodations, too?
- Instructional accommodations are designed to help students learn, so why should they be carried into assessments?
- Because the accommodations research base is not very clear, shouldn't we just allow as many accommodations as possible during instruction and assessment?

Accommodations are changes in the way that materials are presented or in the way that students respond, as well as changes in setting, timing, and scheduling. The reason for providing accommodations is that they enable the student to bypass (or partially bypass) the effects of a disability, so that the student can learn or demonstrate knowledge and skills. Examples of some accommodations that fall within each of these categories are shown in Box 4.1. The goal of this chapter (and of other chapters to follow) is to assist you in becoming a sound decision maker about accommodations.

Box 4.1

Examples of Six Types of Assessment Accommodations

Setting	*Timing*
<ul><li>Individual</li><li>Small group</li><li>Study carrel</li><li>Separate location</li><li>Room with special lighting</li><li>Adaptive or special furniture</li><li>Room with special acoustics</li><li>Minimal distractions environment</li></ul>	<ul><li>Extended time</li><li>Flexible schedule</li><li>Frequent breaks during testing</li><li>Frequent breaks on one subtest but not another</li></ul>

Presentation	*Response*
<ul><li>Audio</li><li>Braille edition</li><li>Large print</li><li>Audio amplification devices, hearing aids</li><li>Noise buffers</li><li>Prompts on tape</li><li>Increased space between items</li><li>Fewer items per page</li><li>Simplify language in directions</li><li>Highlight verbs in instructions by underlining</li><li>One complete sentence per line in reading passages</li><li>Keywords or key phrases in directions highlighted</li><li>Sign directions to student</li><li>Read directions to student</li><li>Reread directions for each page of questions</li><li>Multiple choice questions followed by answer down side with bubbles to right</li><li>Clarify directions</li><li>Cues (arrows, stop signs) on answer form</li><li>Provide additional examples</li><li>Visual magnification devices</li><li>Templates to reduce visible print</li></ul>	<ul><li>Mark in response booklet</li><li>Use brailler</li><li>Tape-record for later verbatim translation</li><li>Use of scribe</li><li>Word processor</li><li>Communication device</li><li>Copying assistance between drafts</li><li>Adaptive or special furniture</li><li>Dark or heavy raised lines</li><li>Pencil grips</li><li>Large diameter pencil</li><li>Calculator</li><li>Abacus</li><li>Arithmetic tables</li><li>Spelling dictionary</li><li>Spell-checker</li><li>Paper secured to work area with tape/magnets</li></ul>

Scheduling	*Other*
<ul><li>Specific time of day</li><li>Subtests in different order</li><li>Across multiple days</li></ul>	<ul><li>Special test preparation</li><li>On-task/focusing prompts</li><li>Others that do not fit into other categories</li></ul>

SOURCE: This table is a reproduction of Box 3.2, Examples of Six Types of Assessment Accommodations, with permission from Thurlow, M. L., Elliott, J. L., & Ysseldyke, J. E. (2003), *Testing students with disabilities: Complying with district and state requirements* (2nd ed.). Thousand Oaks, CA: Corwin.

The kinds of accommodations that are easiest to understand and justify are those that are typically provided to students who have sensory or physical disabilities. For example, the need to magnify instructional materials so that students who have significant visual impairments can see them is obvious. Similarly, it is easy to respect the need for students who have hearing impairments to be provided with amplification equipment, such as hearing aids, so that they can benefit from instruction. These kinds of accommodations are akin to those that are provided to individuals with wheelchairs—without an elevator (or a chair lift), these individuals do not have access to instruction that is provided on the second floor of a building. In the same way, individuals who have difficulty seeing or hearing do not have access to instruction that is provided visually or orally, unless they can use accommodations.

These same arguments apply (but are more difficult to understand) for individuals who have less obvious disabilities, such as learning disabilities, emotional disabilities, and mild mental retardation. Teachers (and others) may sometimes say, "Accommodations are nothing but a crutch. Johnny is just lazy. He could do it if he wanted to do it." When disabilities are less obvious, they are more difficult to recognize—and it is more difficult to realize that the student's access to learning is impeded in much the same way as for students who have visual or hearing impairments.

In Box 4.2, we have an illustration of a student, Kyle, who has a learning disability and struggles to access the curriculum in the same way that other students do. Also illustrated in the example is how accommodations can increase the student's access to the curriculum and how the resulting classroom performance better reflects the student's knowledge and skills than nonaccommodated learning.

Kyle's situation is just one example of a common message about accommodations—that is, accommodations are not about changing the standard of performance. They are about addressing the student's disability needs so that the student's knowledge and skills on the standards being measured can be more validly assessed. The quotation of Maggie McLaughlin, a well-known researcher, is relevant here. She stated about a student who had a reading disability and who needed to be assessed on grade-level content: "He may read at the second-grade level, but that doesn't mean he thinks at the second-grade level." Accommodations enable students to demonstrate what they know and can do without compromising the standards that are being assessed.

This chapter addresses questions of how to make sound decisions about which accommodations a student might need during instruction or assessment. To start, we make a distinction between opinions about accommodations and research-based knowledge. Then, we identify some considerations to ponder before making accommodation decisions for both classroom instruction and assessments. Following this section, we delve into making decisions about accommodations that are needed for instruction and for classroom tests. Finally, we suggest ways to roll instructional and classroom test accommodations into district or state assessments. In conclusion, we address several related issues, such as how to be sure that accommodation information is connected to the Individualized Education Program (IEP) and strategies for assisting students when current accommodations policies are not consistent with student needs.

Box 4.2

Kyle's Access to the General Education Curriculum With and Without Accommodations

Kyle was first diagnosed as having a learning disability in third grade. His reading skills were poor, but his math computation skills were excellent. He had trouble listening to the teacher and to classroom discussions, and he never seemed to be able to complete assignments when he was in the classroom. Sometimes when he bothered other students and kept them from doing their work, Kyle was sent into the hallway, where he was carefully watched by a hall monitor. Here, he could do his work without distraction. Despite his quick completion of tasks, particularly if they were math problems, he was made to stay in the hallway as punishment. As a result, he missed discussions between the teacher and his classmates as they reviewed how problems were solved or how word problems were comprehended.

When the IEP team met for Kyle's annual review, it became obvious that something was not working right. Despite his excellent math skills, Kyle was not enjoying the same access to the curriculum as his classmates. The IEP team identified several accommodations to restore and upgrade his access to the general curriculum.

First, being sent to the hallway to work undistracted was no longer used to help focus on his math problems (nor as punishment). Instead, Kyle was assigned to a carrel in the classroom where he could work undistracted if he needed it. Kyle was taught to figure out when he needed an accommodation to help him work undistracted. Also, to help Kyle pay attention during teacher instruction, he was given a desk at the front of the room, slightly ahead of other students so that he could not bother them. He also was given instruction in self-regulation skills, so that he monitored whether he was on task, and was rewarded for bringing himself back on task (or for remaining on task without redirection).

With these instructional accommodations, Kyle rarely missed teacher instruction or review and discussion periods. Also, he resumed his excellent math performance. As he regained his skills and began again to surpass his classmates, Kyle was allowed to help other students (as long as he remained on task). Because he had access to the general education curriculum, his skills and behavior demonstrated that it was good not only for him but also for his classmates. Also, as a result of the careful consideration of what accommodations would work and which ones he would need to be taught, Kyle gained skills in knowing when he needed accommodations and asking for those that he needed when he needed them.

Making decisions about accommodations might sound simple, given what we have said thus far. But these decisions are far from simple. Many people have struggled with how to make good decisions about accommodations. This ability is a skill, like most others, that is improved through information and practice. The benefits of making good decisions about accommodations are great. Students have access, as they should, to the content that is conveyed by instruction—and they are then able to demonstrate their true knowledge and skills. Skill building takes practice. Certainly, if we expect that students must practice to learn things well, then we (as teachers or administrators) also should be expected to learn by engaging in sufficient practice.

OPINIONS VERSUS RESEARCH-BASED KNOWLEDGE ON ACCOMMODATIONS

In the early 1980s, research was conducted by two large test development companies: ACT and Educational Testing Service (ETS). For several reasons, the relevance of this research to state and district tests is limited. For example, the ACT and ETS research included only limited samples of students (those who were headed for college), and most of the research lumped together disabilities that probably needed to be studied separately, such as physical disabilities and learning disabilities. Commonly cited findings from this research about reasonable time extensions (e.g., up to one and one-half times the standard testing time) may not apply to state and district assessments, especially because most are untimed. We needed new research involving state and district tests before we could develop guiding principles like those from the college entrance testing work.

In the mid-1990s, policymakers realized the need for additional research focused directly on state and district assessments. The U.S. Department of Education provided funds for this research in the hope that it would answer many of the questions that surrounded the use of accommodations during district and state assessments. Although this research is still ongoing, to a great extent the research has revealed that the effects of accommodations are complicated—varying as a function of the test, the characteristics of the student, and attitudes about what accommodations should accomplish.

In Box 4.3, we summarize some of the major findings about accommodations from recent research syntheses. These syntheses make clear that there are many complexities in the findings of the research on the effects of accommodations—even under the best of conditions. Another body of research on accommodations has looked at the implementation of accommodations during the assessment and, somewhat less frequently, in relation to instructional accommodations. Challenges in carrying the accommodations identified by the IEP team into the instructional setting and into the testing setting have been documented by several researchers, with logistical constraints often taking precedence over IEP decisions. Complicating matters is the fact that although states have worked away on getting policies in place, they have devoted less attention to providing training sessions or materials to those who need them, so that there is often a huge disconnect between what the state policies or guidelines are and what districts and schools know about or have access to. These problems are ones that are solvable, and dramatic differences have been documented in the accommodations expertise of teachers in different districts, supposedly a result of differences in training and other supports provided to teachers and IEP teams. Several studies in the past pointed to a tendency toward *overaccommodation* of students who have disabilities. In other words, when making decisions about the accommodations a student would use during an assessment, there was a tendency to pick nearly every accommodation possible—with the mistaken belief that accommodations might increase the student's score, and so the more, the better. This tendency was revealed in research conducted by the National Center for Education Statistics and suggested by other research as well. Research has now confirmed that the unneeded accommodations might actually interfere with a student's performance.

Box 4.3

Summary of Selected Research Syntheses on Accommodations

Bolt, S., & Thurlow, M. L. (2004). Five of the most frequently allowed testing accommodations in state policy. *Remedial and Special Education, 25*(3), 141–152.

In this article, the authors report on the findings from a searchable database on accommodations most often allowed in state policies: dictated response, large print, Braille, extended time, and sign language interpreter for instructions. The summary of research from 36 studies revealed that there were not simple or conclusive answers to questions about the effects of specific accommodations. Suggestions for additional needed research and the nature of the research are provided.

Sireci, S. G., Li, S., & Scarpati, S. (2002). The effects of test accommodation on test performance: A review of the literature. *Center for Educational Assessment Research Report No. 485.* (Available on the Web site of the National Center on Educational Outcomes at www.nceo.info)

In this report, the authors summarize the literature on testing accommodations for students with disabilities and English language learners. After identifying 150 studies on the topic, they determined that 40 studied the effects on performance empirically, and so these were included in the review and critiqued in relation to an interaction hypothesis that argues that test accommodations should improve the test scores of the targeted group but not those of the nontargeted group. Across the wide array of studies reviewed, with many different accommodations included, the one accommodation that seemed to have a fairly consistent finding was extended time. It improved the performance of students with disabilities more than students without disabilities. This paper suggests a revision of the interaction hypothesis as well as providing directions for future research and improved test development and administration practices.

Thompson, S., Blount, A., & Thurlow, M. L. (2002). A summary of research on the effects of test accommodations: 1999 through 2001. *Synthesis Report 34.* (Available at the NCEO Web site www.nceo.info)

This report summarizes 46 empirical research studies that were published from 1999 through 2001, including summary information on the purpose of the studies; the types of assessments, content areas, and accommodations studied; the participants included; the research designs used; the findings; and the limitations of the studies. The report identified many areas of needed clarification in research, such as better definitions of the constructs tested and greater clarity of the accommodations needed by the students themselves. This research synthesis is expected to be updated again in 2005.

Tindal, G., & Fuchs, L. (1999). *Summary of research on test changes: An empirical basis for defining accommodations.* (Available at Mid-South Regional Resource Center Web site http://www.ihdi.uky.edu/msrrc/PDF/Tindal&Fuchs.PDF)

This report provides an analysis and summary of research on test changes, in the broadest sense of the phrase, organized according to changes in schedule, presentation, test directions, use of assistive devices, and setting. The report examined the nature of the research that was conducted and concluded that there was a need for more experimental research on the effects of accommodations. Most research that had been concluded was descriptive or comparative in nature.

Recently there has been some concern that there may also be underaccommodation occurring—especially when there is a great deal of testing going on and the logistics of providing accommodations just seem to become too difficult. Examination of state databases that include information on the use of accommodations suggests that underaccommodation is most likely to occur at the high school level, somewhat less likely at the middle school level, and least likely at the elementary school level. Other reasons for underaccommodation that have occurred more recently are the negative effects and penalties that are assigned to some changes that have been designated by the state as nonstandard accommodations or "modifications"—changes in test administration procedures or materials that affect the construct being measured. In some states, these accommodations result in lower scores, often the lowest score possible, which translates into "penalties" in the eyes of school officials who are trying to ensure that they meet the criteria for adequate yearly progress (AYP) that their state has set under No Child Left Behind (NCLB).

Court Cases and Settlements

Another opinion that has played a part in accommodations policies—and probably will continue to do so—is reflected in court cases and settlements. Recent cases are the most interesting here because they have occurred within the standards-based reform context. Of the four cases brought during the late 1990s and early 2000s, one was decided in favor of the state, two reached settlements, and one is still in process. The first, a case in Indiana, involved a lawsuit brought on behalf of students who were failing the graduation exams because, according to the case, they had not had sufficient time to prepare, and they were not adequately accommodated. The suit was decided on the basis of the adequate time concern, with the rationale that three years is enough time for any student to prepare for a high school exam.

The two cases that settled were in Oregon (*Advocates for Special Kids v. Oregon State Board of Education*) and Alaska (*Disability Rights Advocates v. Alaska*). Both challenged their respective states' assessments for multiple reasons, particularly around concerns about whether students with learning disabilities had equal opportunity to participate in and attain all the benefits of the statewide assessment system. Of special concern was that the states' lists of allowable accommodations were too narrow, and the research base for the policies was nonexistent. The suits argued that accommodations should be allowed if they are consistent with instructional and classroom accommodations and written in the student's IEP—unless the accommodation specifically invalidates the construct and purpose of the test. Both Oregon and Alaska reached settlement agreements that opened up their accommodations policies, as well as clarified the need for clearer policies and procedures surrounding the selection of accommodations, approval of accommodations not listed, and a host of other considerations.

California has a court case still pending. Disability Rights Advocates (DRA), the firm that filed the Oregon and Alaska suits, filed a class action lawsuit in California in May 2001 (*Juleus Chapman et al. v. California Department of Education*) on several grounds, one of which was the accommodations issue—failure of the state to implement effective standards and procedures for ensuring that students with disabilities could obtain reasonable accommodations. Students are now allowed to take the California High School Exit Exam (CAHSEE) with the accommodations listed on their IEPs or 504 accommodation plans (Section 504 of the Rehabilitation Act of 1973) until either a settlement is reached or the court case is decided.

CONSIDERATIONS IN MAKING DECISIONS ABOUT ACCOMMODATIONS

Despite the complexities of the findings, the research does point to the need to make careful and informed decisions about accommodations and to identify the considerations that inform our decision making. With these concepts as a foundation, we can achieve the purpose of this chapter—to help you and your colleagues make sound, supported decisions about accommodations. These decisions will not only hold up to scrutiny by administrators and parents, but they will also be the best decisions for the students. We will list and briefly discuss each consideration.

Consideration: Whether an accommodation is needed and what accommodation is needed should *not* be determined by the student's category of disability.

The clues provided by the disability category are as follows:

- If the student has a sensory disability, it is almost certain that some kind of accommodation will be needed.
- In all categories, the more severe the disability, the more likely the student is to need an accommodation.

Disability categories provide only some clues about the need for accommodations or the specific accommodations needed. The disability category never should be used as the sole basis for deciding that a student does or does not need an accommodation or what accommodation is needed. Decisions about specific accommodations needed by a student always must start with a consideration of the student as an individual; in other words, consider what the student's learning and behavior characteristics and skills are. Take the example of students who are easily distracted (regardless of their specific category of disability). When thinking about accommodations, it is useful to think about whether changes are needed to address organizational issues (such as providing a highlighter or template), timing issues (such as providing frequent breaks), setting issues (such as locating the student in the front of the classroom), or a combination of these and other issues. This is a very individualized decision-making process.

Consideration: Whether an accommodation is needed and what specific accommodation is needed should *not* be determined by the availability of accommodations.

Starting from available accommodations and then determining whether students need them is a backward approach to deciding on the need for accommodations. Clear reasons exist for decision making to proceed in the other direction—to start from student characteristics and needs—and on the basis of this information to determine whether accommodations are needed in instruction, classroom tests, and district and state assessments.

Making decisions about accommodations by starting with the student's needs is more difficult with some tests than with others. Criterion-referenced tests (CRTs), in which student performance is compared to a criterion that is to be reached, seem to be more accommodation friendly than norm-referenced tests (NRTs) in which student performance is compared to the performance of other students. When between-student comparisons are made, the mind-set of test developers (and many test administrators) is that all students must take the test exactly the same way. We are not saying that this mind-set is incorrect, but it should be recognized and countered if a student truly cannot accurately show his or her knowledge and skills without a needed accommodation. Even though more and more students with disabilities are included in standardization samples, with needed accommodations, the use of "nonapproved" accommodations when taking CRTs continues to be an issue. This issue must continue to be debated and solved for students who have disabilities.

Basing accommodations decisions on the availability of specific accommodations could be interpreted as a violation of federal law, because this process might result in an individual not being provided a necessary accommodation. Thus, availability should never be a consideration when identifying which specific accommodations a student might need. The time to consider availability of accommodation is when you are figuring out the *logistics* of providing accommodations to students. Sometimes, this task can be quite a challenge. Nevertheless, this process should not be a consideration during decision making about specific accommodations that individual students need.

Consideration: Whether an accommodation is needed and the specific accommodations that are needed by a student might change over time as a function of the student's age or skills.

This concept is sometimes difficult to understand. In fact, you might have been taught that once an individual has a disability, that disability is there to stay. This belief might also be bolstered by some research that has concluded that once students are placed in special education services, they almost never escape from them. But day-to-day reality suggests that this situation is not always the case. Many students' particular needs can and do change over time.

Improvements in students' skills and a greater maturity both probably play a role in the possible change in whether a student needs accommodations and in the specific accommodations that are needed. Think about what happens to people who need glasses. As they get older, their vision disability does change, in that the need for far vision assistance usually decreases with age, while the need for near vision assistance usually increases.

Just as the decision about whether a student needs any accommodations may change over time, so may the decision about specific accommodations that are needed. To understand this point, let's go back to the example of what happens to people who need glasses. Although a person's vision disability can change over time such that there is a need for magnification rather than far vision assistance, during the same period of time a need for amplification equipment for hearing might be needed, although this equipment was not previously needed. Maturation and skill development can affect the specific accommodations needs of youngsters, just as they obviously affect the assistance needs of those who are older.

Consideration: Whether an accommodation is needed, and the specific accommodations that are needed, should *not* be determined by how well a student is performing.

There may be a tendency among school personnel to think that low student performance is a surefire way to determine whether an accommodation is needed. This statement is not necessarily true. Similarly, the fact that a student is performing well in class and on tests is not a surefire indication that the student does not need an accommodation. Students can perform poorly simply because they have never been exposed to the general education curriculum or a particular content area. They are not going to perform better just by receiving accommodations. For example, providing extended time to a student who has not been exposed to the curriculum that is being tested is not likely to improve test performance. Similarly, students who perform well in the classroom and during tests might be doing so despite their disabilities. Their performance, although high, might be much lower than it would be if they were provided the needed accommodations.

Still, one of the most obvious signs of the need for accommodations is probably poor performance. The poor performance, however, must be linked to some obvious limitation in behavior or skill that interferes with demonstrating other skills.

SELECTING ACCOMMODATIONS FOR INSTRUCTION AND CLASSROOM TESTS

The considerations that we just highlighted serve as reminders that decisions about accommodations—especially those concerning specific accommodations that are needed—must be individualized. They should not be made for groups of students; rather, they should be made for specific students based on their learning and behavior characteristics and skills.

Box 4.4 shows a list of several common instructional accommodations. In addition, many of these are used during classroom tests. We do not mean, however, that they can be *directly* used during district and state tests. Some instructional accommodations should not be used in the testing situation. For example, during reading instruction, an appropriate accommodation might be to read along with the student, perhaps having the student follow along as someone reads to him or her. When the student is taking a reading test that is designed to assess decoding skills, then the read-along accommodation is not appropriate. Making decisions about what accommodations confuse the construct that is being measured requires a good understanding of the test. More about this subject will appear in Chapter 5.

Although the easiest approach to deciding what accommodations a student will use during instruction and during classroom tests is to start from a checklist of all possible accommodations, that approach generally fosters overaccommodation. Likely, this action will result in identifying accommodations that are only minimally related to the student's needs.

Box 4.4

Common Instructional Accommodations, A to Z

Altered assignments

Audiotaped directions

Bold print

Bulletin board strategy reminders

Color coding

Crib notes

Darker lines

Directions clarified or simplified

Enlarged materials

Extended time

Fewer tasks per assignment

Finger spacing, counting strategies

Graph paper for calculations

Green color as cue to continue

Harder items first

Headphones

Individual work area

Isolated items

Keywords highlighted

Knock-on-desk cues

Large pictures

Limit number of tasks

Manipulatives

Memory aids

Natural supports

Note-taking aids

On-task reminders

Outline text

Paper holders (magnets, tape, etc.)

Peer support

Quality monitoring

Questions in margins

Reader

Raised print

Shorter assignments

Seat location change

Touch talker (communication device)

Tutoring (cross-age, peer)

Underline key points

Use reminders

Visual prompts

Vocabulary cues on paper or board

Wider margins

Word list on board

Word processor

X-out text to reduce reading

Yellow paper

Zero-wrong strategies

Steps to Take in Identifying Accommodations for Individual Students

You can take several steps to identify the accommodations that individual students need for classroom instruction and classroom tests. These steps include the following:

- Ask the students, individually, about what helps them learn better. What gets in the way of them showing what they really know and can do?
- Ask parents about the things that they do to help their child complete household tasks or homework. Often, parents and other family members have wonderful insights about needed accommodations, although they may not use the term *accommodations*.
- Consider the strengths and weaknesses of students in areas linked to the curriculum. Identify those skills or behaviors that seem to consistently get in the way of learning.
- Teach students how to use accommodations that might be provided. You should do this task to determine whether a particular accommodation really is needed by a particular student. Making this determination is impossible if the student does not know how to use an accommodation.
- Observe the effects of provided accommodations to determine whether the accommodation is being used and the extent to which the accommodation seems to be useful to students.
- Collect data on the effects of accommodations that are used by individual students. With the current lack of concrete research data on the effects of accommodations in general, there must be a more objective way to judge the effects of accommodations for individual students, not just through observations of whether they seem to make a difference. Simple curriculum-based measures might be the easiest and the most accurate way to get this kind of information.

These steps and others are incorporated into a worksheet for your use (refer to Box 4.5). We discuss each of these steps in a little more detail here, because they are so critical for making sound accommodations decisions.

Ask the Student

Students are usually knowledgeable about what helps them perform better on tests. Although they might be better able to explain their needs as they age, even young students have ideas about what does and does not help them. Gathering the information might have to be done in slightly different ways, but it is possible to obtain.

Among the questions that you will want to ask students are the following (refer to the questionnaire in Box 4.6). Remember to adjust the questions for students of different ages.

- The format of the test is [indicate the format]. Do you think that this format will be okay for you, or is there some way that the format could be changed to help you perform your best on the test?

Box 4.5

Classroom Accommodations Worksheet

Follow these steps to identify accommodations that are needed for classroom instruction and for classroom tests for a specific student. Be sure to consider the specific characteristics, strengths, and weaknesses of the student for whom this worksheet is being completed. For each step, be sure to separately consider instruction and tests, and use the questions to spark ideas about useful accommodations. You will find it helpful to complete this worksheet with other individuals who know the student.

	Reflections on Each Question	Possible Instructional Accommodations	Possible Classroom Test Accommodations
1. What helps the student learn better or perform better? What gets in the way of the student showing what he or she really knows and can do?			
2. What have the student's parents or guardian told you about things that they do to help the student complete household tasks or school homework?			
3. What are the student's strengths and weaknesses? What skills or behaviors often get in the way of learning or performance?			
4. What accommodations has the student been taught to use? Are there other accommodations on which the student needs training?			
5. For which accommodations have effects been observed? What accommodations is the student willing to use?			
6. Have any quantitative data (e.g., from one-minute tests) been collected on the effects of accommodations?			
7. Is there any other relevant information that might affect the provision of accommodations, either during classroom instruction or during tests?			

Box 4.6

Student Accommodations Questionnaire

Students often are the best source of information about accommodations that they need and that they are willing to use (the two are not always the same). Students' skills at answering questions about their accommodations needs are naturally better as they mature. Still, being able to identify needed accommodations is an important skill for students who have disabilities (and is a skill that can be developed). By asking students questions about accommodations (using a different term) even at young ages, you will help students hone their skills in identifying needed accommodations (as well as clue you in to important information).

The following questions can be used to ask students about accommodations. Be sure first that you understand the assessment that students will be taking so that you can convey this information to the student. Adjust your vocabulary and question complexity for the age of the student.

- Do you think that the test [describe for the student] will be okay for you, or is there some way that it could be changed to help you perform your best?
- Is there anything about the content of the test or what it asks you to do [describe for the student] that could be changed to help you perform your best?
- Is there anything about the test's timing procedures [describe for the student] that could be changed to help you perform your best?
- Is there anything about when the test is given [describe for the student] that could be changed to help you perform your best?
- Is there anything about the way the test is presented [describe for the student] that could be changed to help you perform your best?
- Is there anything about how you have to answer the test [describe for the student] that could be changed to help you perform your best?
- Is there anything about the test that could be changed to help you perform your best on the test?

- The timing of this test is [insert information about how the test is timed]. Is there anything about the timing procedures that could be changed to help you perform your best on the test?
- The test is scheduled to occur [indicate when in the day or week that the test is scheduled]. Is there any way that this scheduling could be changed to help you perform your best on the test?
- The test is typically presented in the following manner [indicate the manner of test administration]. Is there any way that the presentation format could be changed to help you perform your best on the test?
- The test typically enables you to respond to the test by [indicate the test-response methods]. Is there any way that this response format could be changed to help you perform your best on the test?
- Are there any other changes in the assessment that could help you perform your best on the test?

These questions can be adjusted for younger children by giving examples of some possible accommodations that fit within each of the types of accommodations. For older students, the questions can be merged into one general question about whether there are any changes in testing that would not change what is measured, but which would help the student perform better.

Ask Parents and Other Family Members

Parents spend a lot of time with their children—time during which they pick up cues as to what helps their children learn and what interferes with their learning. While parents might not necessarily use the word *accommodations*, they can respond to questions that describe the essence of accommodations. For example, they usually know whether providing directions one time is enough for their child to understand what is to be done. They usually know whether there are ways to tune in the attention of the child to obtain the best performance possible. They often know what times during the day the student will perform best and when the student's downtime occurs.

Consider Strengths and Weaknesses

Accommodations that a student needs are determined by individual student characteristics. Perhaps one of the easiest ways to determine what these needs are is to examine the student's strengths and weaknesses. The weaknesses help focus on what characteristics might interfere with showing knowledge and skills. These are the factors that accommodations are needed for to *bypass* the disability. Examining the student's strengths is also advantageous, because you can see the characteristics on which accommodations can capitalize.

For example, if a student is easily distracted, that student's adequate math skills might be hidden because of the student's inability to complete items under standard test conditions. Yet, this same student might have good skills in organizing materials, keeping track of what is next in sequences, and so on. Although we typically think of accommodations such as extended time and breaks for students who are easily distracted, for the student in our example, there are some additional logical approaches to bypassing the effect of distraction. One way is to build on the strength of organization and sequencing to develop a template that covers everything but the problem on which the student is working. Because the student has skills in sequencing and organization, the student will be able to move the template down the page as each problem is completed—and, at the same time, curb the effects of distraction.

Teach the Use of Accommodations

Much discussion has occurred about the need for accommodations that are used during assessment to be accommodations that the student has received during instruction. Some places, in fact, have made it a requirement that an accommodation be used in instruction for at least three months before the accommodation can be used in an assessment. The message is that students must be used to using accommodations before they use them in assessments.

An implicit assumption is that if accommodations have been used during instruction, then the student knows how to use them. This statement could not be farther from the truth. Simply providing accommodations to students during instruction does not ensure that the students really know how to use them.

Students need to be directly taught how to use accommodations and the best ways to use them. This lesson is obvious for certain accommodations. For example, students must be taught how to read Braille before it is a reasonable accommodation for them to use during assessment. Although the need for instruction on the use of an accommodation is relatively clear here, the need is less obvious for some accommodations, such as using a template or playing a tape recorder to read directions to the students. If a student has not been directly instructed on how best to use these accommodations, these accommodations might be misused, and their effects might not be what was originally intended.

Observe the Effects of Accommodations

Making sure that the student has been instructed in how best to use accommodations still does not ensure that any of the accommodations will be effective. To document that accommodations are having the intended effects, you should collect data about their effects.

One way to collect data is to observe the effects of accommodations. Anecdotal comments about what was observed are at best only satisfactory for this purpose. The more that the observations can be systematized and recorded, the better the data. In order words, you need to show the impact of the accommodation.

Collect Data About the Effects of Accommodations

Observational data can be useful in documenting the effects of accommodations. Even better are data that are more objective, such as collecting direct measures of performance. Simple measures that are repeated over time can serve this function. These simple measures are one- to three-minute mini-tests (also known as curriculum-based measures) in which the student either reads words or passages, computes the answers to calculation problems, or writes for one minute in response to a sentence prompt. The number of words read, problems solved, or words written composes the data that can be used to judge the effectiveness of accommodations. Comparing performance on these simple measures with and without the use of specific accommodations gives good individual data concerning the effects of the accommodations.

An example of a chart format to keep track of the effects of accommodations is shown in Box 4.7 (also refer to Chapter 7 on instruction). A case study in which these kinds of data are tracked is provided in Box 4.8. As you will notice, data are collected first before any accommodations are used and then again after the introduction of an accommodation on which the student has received instruction. Finally, data are again collected with the student not using the accommodation. In this way, you have a specific documentation of effects—and therefore, information about the student's need for the particular accommodation.

Box 4.7

Tracking the Effects of Accommodations

Charting the performance of a student on the same type of task (e.g., reading a list of words) when using one or more accommodations (and without the accommodations) provides an excellent way to track the effects of accommodations. This task can be done easily by having the student spend one to five minutes on the task. On some days, the student has no accommodations, and on other days, the student uses an accommodation. By charting the performance on a graph and noting when accommodations are used and when they are not used, you can easily obtain a good picture of whether the accommodation has an effect on the student's performance.

The following is the type of chart that can easily be drawn on graph paper and used to track the effects of one or more accommodations.

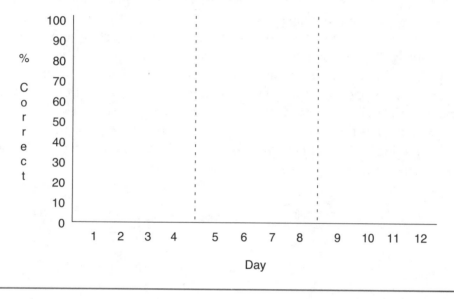

Rolling Classroom Accommodations Into District and State Assessments

The information that you gathered through quick administration measures provides useful evidence of the need for an accommodation to carry over from the classroom into district and state assessments. In addition to having evidence of the need for an accommodation, you (and anyone who is questioning the need for an accommodation) will find it helpful to document the accommodations that a student is receiving and will need during state and district assessments. We recommend using a simple form, something like what is provided in Box 4.9, to show where a student is receiving which accommodations. Thus, as shown in the example in Box 4.9, a student might receive the same accommodation in instruction, classroom assessment, district assessments, and state assessments. Or, alternately, a student might receive a specific accommodation in all situations except the state assessment. Whenever a discrepancy in the alignment occurs, we recommend that

Box 4.8

Case Study on Tracking the Effects of Accommodations

Ms. Jones decides that Mao needs to use accommodations during the state test. She already uses several accommodations for Mao during instruction, but Ms. Jones has never checked them out in any systematic way. Because she knows about the tendency to overaccommodate and recognizes the finding that overaccommodation sometimes impedes performance, she has decided to check some of the accommodations that she uses with Mao during instruction to see whether they really would have an effect during the statewide math assessment, especially the computation section.

Ms. Jones checks the three accommodations during the next three weeks. Every day except Friday, she has Mao take a short, two-minute math calculation test. During the first four days (Week 1), she has Mao take the test with no accommodations. Then, during Week 2, she has Mao take the test under unlimited time conditions. Finally, during Week 3, she has Mao take the test with no accommodations.

The following chart shows the results of Ms. Jones's tracking study. Clearly, the accommodation makes a difference in Mao's performance. The percentage correct that she obtains is much higher when she is tested under unlimited time conditions. The difference is not quite as dramatic as one would initially think, however. By reinstituting testing without accommodations, Ms. Jones sees that Mao's performance is higher the second time without accommodations than the first time. This information might suggest that Mao's performance is increasing because of classroom instruction and the practice she is receiving by simply taking the test.

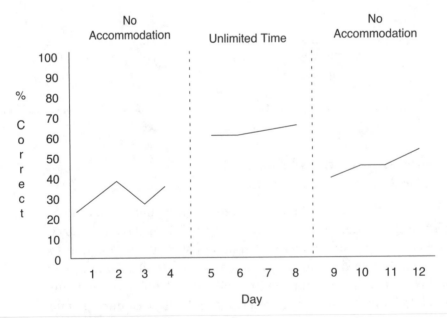

Ms. Jones could gather even more information by tracking more accommodations over a longer period of time. By extending the duration of her tracking, Ms. Jones could also get a better feel for the potential impact of simply providing Mao with practice on test formats and content.

Box 4.9

Form to Determine Links Among Classroom Accommodations, Classroom Testing Accommodations, and District or State Testing Accommodations

Accommodation	Instruction	Classroom Assessment	District Assessment	State Assessment	Reasons for Discrepancy among Columns
Frequent breaks	X	X	X	X	
Read text to student	X	X	X		Policy does not allow instate test and student wants to take the test without accommodations.

you document the reason for the discrepancy among the situations in which an accommodation can be used.

Despite your documentation of accommodations and the alignment in where they are used, it is still possible that questions will be raised about certain accommodations. If the test publisher or others raise questions about whether an accommodation gives the student an advantage that other students do not receive, and in your opinion it is essential that the student should use the accommodations, then you should provide the student the needed accommodation and enlist the aid of evaluation or assessment personnel within your district to back you up if necessary.

Evaluation or assessment personnel in your district potentially can engage in a study of collecting data from comparison students who also are provided the accommodation, although they do not need it. The purpose of performing this task is to determine whether the effect of the accommodation for the student who needs it is different from the effect of the accommodation for students who do not need it. A differential effect is typically taken as evidence of the need for the accommodation for the student who has the disability.

Remember, asking for help to have someone double-check the effects of an accommodation really is needed only to carry questionable accommodations into state or district assessments. For these tests (both NRTs and CRTs), you will have to be able to support the need for specific accommodations.

A WORD ABOUT TECHNOLOGY ACCOMMODATIONS

Technology is expected to solve many of today's problems. This statement is true for instruction and assessment, just as it is true for business. We already are making use of more common technology, such as tape recorders, self-timers, communication boards, and word processors.

Lately, researchers have begun to realize that computers can aid test taking by providing accommodations through the computer medium. In a press release, Dr. Martha Burk (a researcher and software developer) stated, "We have . . . shown that computers are capable of producing the types of accommodations that are often recommended for these students, and such accommodations can also raise test scores." Among the accommodations that the computer version of a test could easily provide to students were large print, extra spacing, and sound. In addition to better performance, Dr. Burk reported that the computerized testing helped students feel "more confident in taking the tests—even when their computer experience was limited or nonexistent."

The possibilities are blossoming. We now see computer presentation of some instruction opening tremendous possibilities for providing students who have disabilities access to the general education curriculum. This goal is achieved, for example, by incorporating definitions of terms, explanations of assumed background information, and a variety of other avenues within the text to widen access to the curriculum. The possibilities for likewise opening testing to provide access to students who have disabilities are being explored through new research efforts.

FACING SOME ACCOMMODATIONS REALITIES

As if making decisions about accommodations was not tough enough, there are several complications with the use of accommodations. We identify and address three of these complications here: IEP documentation issues, nonapproved accommodations, and an appeals process. We provide this information primarily to alert you. The specifics for each of these topics will vary with your district and state policies.

IEP Documentation Issues

Documenting accommodations to be provided in instruction is no longer an option. This information has been required since enactment of the Individuals With Disabilities Education Act of 1997 (IDEA 97) to be documented on the IEP.

The accommodations to be provided during district and state assessments also must be documented.

Because IEP teams typically meet in the fall, in the late spring, or sometimes even year-round, decisions are often made far from the time of district and state assessments. Much can happen during that time period, and one of the things that typically does happen is that different accommodations needs emerge or are identified. In other words, the IEP team must meet again so that the proper accommodations can be documented.

No easy ways exist to get around this requirement. Simply indicating that the student can have every accommodation that is allowed by the district or the state policy is not an appropriate action to take. We already know that over-accommodation should be avoided, in large part because the use of accommodations that are not needed might actually interfere with the student's best performance.

The requirement to document accommodations on IEPs and to reconvene when changes need to be made actually heightens the importance of making good accommodations decisions at the beginning. Also, this requirement emphasizes the need to base these decisions on data, as suggested in our discussion of instructional accommodations.

Nonapproved Accommodations

Every district and state assessment has policies that identify accommodations that are not acceptable to use during the assessment, because it has been determined that those accommodations change the meaning of the test, the score comparability, or some other important test characteristic. Some policies refer to these unacceptable changes as "modifications," while others simply refer to them as nonstandard accommodations. The specific accommodations that are included in these unacceptable lists vary; different districts and states disapprove different accommodations. We know that one state might recommend an accommodation that another state specifically disapproves.

The critical questions are these: What are you supposed to do if the student really needs one of these nonapproved accommodations to even have access to taking the test? Should you force the student to not use the needed accommodation so that the student's score will count? Should you provide the needed accommodation and not worry about whether the student's score counts? And, if counting means not graduating, can you legally perform this action?

We would argue that what you do has to depend on the purpose of the test—whether it is used for system or student accountability. If the test has implications for system accountability only, the student should be permitted to use the needed accommodation. But you should make sure that if the student uses the accommodation, that student's score still counts. If, for some reason, a student's score is not reflected in aggregated data, you should still obtain information on how the student performed. Further, you should obtain aggregated data for all students whose scores are not reflected in the district or state reporting system. As we write this book, NCLB guidance is about to be released that may address the issues of nonstandard accommodations. Because many students with disabilities need these accommodations, it will be important to attend to the NCLB regulations and guidance.

When it comes to student accountability, the decisions might need to be different. If the use of a particular accommodation is not allowed and the student's score will not count toward passing a graduation exam if the accommodation is used, then the student and the student's parents need to make some tough decisions. Among their choices are the following: (1) file a lawsuit claiming unfair disadvantage because the accommodation is not allowed, (2) do not use the accommodation and determine whether performance is at a passing level, (3) do Number 2, then if necessary, do Number 1. Another option that may or may not be available in your state or district is to proceed through an appeals process or an alternative route to the standard diploma.

Appeals Processes and Alternative Routes

Many states and some districts now have an appeals process in place for those students who have not been successful in passing a test. Sometimes this appeals process also applies to the use of specific accommodations. It is essential to find out about the appeals process in your district or state and know what procedures must be followed to file an appeal. You must also know what options a successful appeal provides to you and to the student.

In some states, students do not have to first fail the graduation or promotion exam to have access to an alternative route to demonstrating their knowledge and skills. As in those states with an appeals process, the requirements for eligibility to an alternative route differ by state and district, and the specific procedures that students must follow to demonstrate that they have met the requirements vary greatly.

Appeals processes and alternative routes should exist for both graduation exams and for promotion tests that determine whether a student moves from one grade to the next. In reality, because promotion exams are only recently becoming more common, the alternatives that do exist have been developed for graduation decisions. A fairly common approach is to have a criterion for when a student can begin the process (e.g., having not passed the graduation exam at least three times). Then the student typically has to provide alternative evidence of having met the graduation standards. Sometimes this alternative evidence is a portfolio that contains an array of independent student work that shows that the student is meeting these standards. Other times, the alternative evidence is an oral presentation, either to a panel or to an administrator (principal or superintendent) who then makes a recommendation to the school board or other authority.

Often it takes a bit of digging to find information about alternative routes and appeals. They are a challenge to the assessment system. These approaches suggest that the test cannot accurately measure everyone. Thus, their existence is often not advertised or even placed in easily accessed locations. If an alternative route

---

Box 4.10

Case Study on Making Accommodations Decisions for Instruction and Testing

Roberto is a third-grade student who has recently moved into the state from a state that has extremely different educational supports. He now faces school daily with a certain amount of trepidation, because everyone in the school seems to be emphasizing what he cannot do, rather than what he can do. This situation is almost directly opposite of what was happening in his prior school, so he is beginning to question whether he can do what is expected of him. He is personalizing the concerns of teachers and administrators in his new school about his need for a reader (for the math test), extended time (for the reading test), and a spell-checker (for the writing test). Also, as a result, when first asked about what he needed when taking the state test, he indicated that he needed nothing. Nothing is what he got.

His performance was lower than any test score he had ever gotten before. Despite his excellent math skills, he barely finished any items, and those he did complete were mostly wrong.

Luckily, his math teacher had recently attended a seminar on instructional accommodations. There, he learned about what accommodations are, about the controversy that surrounds them, and why they are an important part of providing students who have disabilities with access to instruction. He began making sure that Roberto worked with a peer—sharing the reading of directions and word problems—and then answering questions on his own. He also provided Roberto with tape-recorded homework assignments. With these instructional accommodations, Roberto's math performance soared. He now is showing what he knows and can do without the impediment of his reading disability.

---

or appeals process is needed, however, it is well worth the effort taken to find out about it.

SUMMARY

Accommodations are often an emotional and highly charged issue. Students have the right to appropriate and reasonable accommodations, but each person has a different perspective of what is appropriate and what is reasonable. Although the controversy is important, you should not let it impinge on making the best decisions for students. In this chapter, we have highlighted many of the major considerations to keep in mind, as well as the specifics of starting from instructional accommodations and proceeding to those that can be used during classroom testing—and those that can be used in district and state tests. (Refer to Boxes 4.10 and 4.11 for case studies that exemplify many of these considerations.) As research continues on what is appropriate and reasonable, we must continue to make good decisions for individual students and to implement those decisions well. We hope that this chapter has provided you with steps along this path.

> **Box 4.11**
>
> ### Case Study on Planning Accommodations
>
> **Directions:** Use the case study here to extend your understanding and planning for accommodations.
>
> Iva Haddit is an elementary teacher in Johnny B. Goode Elementary School. In her class of 35 students, she has six resource room students, one 504 plan student, two English language learners, and five Title I students. Many of these students require accommodations to participate in the grade curriculum and assessment program. Iva identifies the accommodation needs of each student. Her intent is to use these accommodations during instruction, on classroom tests, and then finally for the district and state assessments. Although she has 14 special needs students, not all of them need assessment accommodations.
>
> As the result of her student-by-student analysis, Iva summarizes her classroom accommodation needs as follows:
>
> Four students need oral reading of directions and questions (José, Rose, Jimmy, Robert).
> One student needs a written translation of tests into Khmer (Maya).
> Four students need testing in a small group (José, Maya, Jimmy, Paco).
> One student needs more frequent breaks during testing (Kimberly).
>
> *Focus Questions*
>
> 1. What must be done to provide the needed accommodations for the students' classroom instruction and tests as well as for district or state assessments?
>
> 2. What are your strategies for making this happen? Who will need to be involved? Be sure to consider scheduling, location, personnel, and materials.
>
> 3. How will the integrity and implementation of the provided accommodations be monitored?
>
> **Action Plan:** Plan and record your strategy for implementation and delivery of needed accommodations. The logistics of providing accommodations need to be thought out well in advance.

TEST YOUR KNOWLEDGE

Testing your knowledge is a good way to determine what you might need to review before proceeding. Complete the following fill-in-the-blank statements, rereading parts of this chapter when necessary:

1. Making good accommodations decisions is a _____ that can be improved by information and practice.

2. Research on accommodations has revealed that the effects of accommodations are _____, varying as a function of the test, the characteristics of the student, and attitudes about what accommodations should accomplish.

3. Accommodations that are used in instruction should not be determined by the student's disability _____.

4. The availability of accommodations should not be a consideration in determining the accommodations that a student will receive during _____.

5. Changes in students' skills and greater maturity both probably play a role in possible changes in whether a student needs _____.

6. Using a checklist to determine what accommodations a student needs fosters _____.

7. A critical step in accommodations decision making is to _____ the student how to use accommodations.

8. To document that accommodations are having intended effects, it is necessary to _____ _____ on their effects.

9. Computers can aid test taking by providing _____ through the computer medium.

10. If different accommodations needs emerge during the year, the _____ _____ must meet again to discuss accommodations for assessment.

ANSWERS

1. skill (p. 48)

2. complicated (p. 49)

3. category (p. 52)

4. assessments (p. 52)

5. accommodations (p. 53)

6. overaccommodation (p. 54)

7. teach (p. 59)

8. collect data (p. 60)

9. accommodations (p. 64)

10. IEP team (p. 65)

REFLECTIONS ON CHANGE

See Appendix A for the Reflections on Change activity for this chapter (p. 191).

RECOMMENDED RESOURCES

ASES SCASS. (in press). *How to choose and use accommodations for students with disabilities: Professional development for IEP teams.* Washington, DC: Council of State School Officers.

Burk, M. (1999). *Computerized test accommodations: A new approach for inclusion and success for students with disabilities.* Washington, DC: A. U. Software.

Burns, E. (1998). *Test accommodations for students with disabilities.* Springfield, IL: Charles C Thomas.

DeStefano, L., Shriner, J. G., & Lloyd, C. A. (2001). Teacher decision making in participation of students with disabilities in large-scale assessment. *Exceptional Children, 68*(1), 7–22.

Disability Rights Advocates. (2001). *Do no harm—High stakes testing and students with learning disabilities.* Oakland, CA: Author.

Elliott, J. E., & Shrag, J. (2002, February). Assessment and accommodation: Lessons learned in Oregon. *International Dyslexia Association.*

Fuchs, L. S., & Fuchs, D. (1999, November). Fair and unfair testing accommodations. *The School Administrator, 56*(10), 24–29.

Fuchs, L. S., & Fuchs, D. (2001). Helping teachers formulate sound test accommodation decisions for students with learning disabilities. *Learning Disabilities Research and Practice, 16*(3), 174–181.

Fuchs, L. S., Fuchs, D., Eaton, S. B., Hamlett, C., & Karns, K. (2000). Supplementing teacher judgments about test accommodations with objective data sources. *School Psychology Review, 29*(1), 65–85.

Henry, S. (1999, November). Accommodating practices. *The School Administrator, 56*(10), 32–38.

Langley, J., & Olsen, K. (2003). *Training district and state personnel on accommodations: A study of state practices, challenges and resources.* Washington, DC: Council of Chief State School Officers.

Lazarus, S., Thompson, S., & Thurlow, M. (2004). *How students access accommodations in assessment and instruction: Results of a survey of special education teachers* (Issue Brief). College Park, MD: University of Maryland, Educational Policy Reform Research Institute.

Lehr, C., & Thurlow, M. (2003). *Putting it all together: Including students with disabilities in assessment and accountability systems* (Policy Directions 16). Minneapolis, MN: National Center on Educational Outcomes.

National School Boards Association and Office of Special Education Programs. (1997). *Technology for students with disabilities: A decision maker's resource guide.* Washington, DC: U.S. Department of Education.

Rhode Island Department of Education. (2003). *Rhode Island assessment accommodation study: Research summary.* Minneapolis: University of Minnesota, National Center on Educational Outcomes. Retrieved July 10, 2004, from http://education.umn .edu/NCEO/TopicAreas/Accommodations/RhodeIsland/htm

Shriner, J. G., & DeStefano, L. (2003). Participation and accommodation in state assessment: The role of individualized education programs. *Exceptional Children, 69*(2), 147–161.

Sireci, S. G., Li, S., & Scarpati, S. (2003). *The effects of test accommodation on test performance: A review of the literature* (Research Report 485). Amherst, MA: Center for Educational Assessment.

Thompson, S. J., Blount, A., & Thurlow, M. L. (2002). *A summary of research on the effects of test accommodations: 1999 through 2001* (Technical Report 34). Minneapolis: University of Minnesota, National Center on Educational Outcomes.

Thurlow, M. L., Thompson, S. J., & Lazarus, S. (in press). Considerations for the administration of tests to special needs students: Accommodations, modifications, and more. In T. Haladyna & S. Downing (Eds.), *Handbook of test development.*[AU: Please provide page numbers.] Mahwah, NY: Lawrence Erlbaum.

Willingham, W. W., Ragosta, M., Bennett, R. E., Braun, H., Rock, D. A., & Powers, D. E. (Eds.). (1988). *Testing handicapped people.* Boston: Allyn & Bacon.

INTERNET RESOURCES

Center for Applied Special Technology: www.cast.org

Council for Exceptional Children: www.cec.sped.org/

Educational Testing Service: www.ets.org/

Mid-South Regional Resource Center: www.ihdi.uky.edu/msrrc

National Center on Educational Outcomes (NCEO): www.nceo.info

National Center for Education Statistics (NCES): http://nces.ed.gov

National Center for Research on Evaluation, Standards, and Student Testing: http://cresst96.cse.ucla.edu/index.html

National Association of Test Directors: www.natd.org

National Information Center for Children and Youth With Disabilities (NICHCY): www.nichcy.org

Preparing Students for Testing

Give me a fish, and I will eat today. Teach me to fish, and I will eat for a lifetime.

—*Chinese proverb*

Hot-Button Issues

- Is it ethical to use student instructional time just to get students ready to take district and state tests?
- I have to teach the curriculum. I do not have time for this test-taking skills stuff.

Test-taking strategies are just one aspect of preparing students to take classroom, district, and state tests. Several ways are available to prepare students for tests that will also help them to be better students and self-advocates. In addition, these methods will benefit students as they move out of the K–12 system and into the world of work or other postsecondary settings. Preparing students for assessments and working with parents, families, and others to support students to do their best (see Chapter 9) also benefits the educational system as a whole.

Preparation for classroom, district, and state tests is an important aspect of improving students' test performance. Some studies have suggested that scores can improve significantly just from simple instruction in how to prepare for testing. The expectation exists that these types of gains from test preparation will be even more pronounced for students who have disabilities. Although many test-preparation skills may come more naturally to students who do not have disabilities, these skills need to be taught to all students, including students with disabilities.

CAUSES AND CONSIDERATIONS

There are some important, general areas that lead up to and underscore the importance of test preparation, be it for classroom, district, or state assessments. The following sections describe some causes and considerations for lack of test performance:

Lack of Testing Strategies. You know these students when you see them. Think of the student who does not know how to pace himself or herself on an assignment, much less a test. Or the student who is unable to set priorities for completing assignments, much less tests. Or, finally, the student who does not know how to pick off the easy tasks or questions, thereby building momentum to tackle the harder ones? Direct instruction is needed to teach students how to build a timing strategy, as well as for question or task selection and priority setting. Students must be taught and learn how to cope with timed test environments. Time management and self-regulation are frequently mentioned in test preparation books. Of course, these topics are particularly important to students with disabilities, many of whom suffer from poor skills in these areas to begin with. Students need to be taught these strategies and learn how to set priorities in problem solving to choose the most advantageous test questions for them to answer.

In addition, students need to be taught how to value the knowledge of learning how tests are scored or weighted. Think about a classroom test. It is critical for students to know that the essay section, for example, is 60% of their test grade. This should help them prioritize their test-taking time and effort. Students need to learn that by completing the easier questions first, they have a better chance of answering these correctly. They need to learn to leave the difficult ones for last (or not at all). Although not all tests are constructed with easy or hard questions in identifiable places, having the strategies to peruse and prioritize items certainly helps.

Lack of Problem-Solving Skills. A particularly strong feature of tests is the way in which they may test students on material they have been taught, but in a fundamentally different way than students may have learned them. At the most basic level, consider the elementary student who has learned to proficiently master the following:

$$\begin{array}{r} 873 \\ -716 \\ \hline \end{array}$$

However, on the day of testing she is presented with the same mathematical concept but presented in one the following ways: $873 - 716 =$ ___ or solve for *n*: $873 - 716 = n$. Certainly we want to know whether students can solve this problem regardless of how it is presented. Students need to be taught how to put their knowledge into practice in multiple ways. Teaching students problem-solving methods and critical-thinking skills will help!

Lack of Strategies to Address the Psychological Stress That Comes With Testing. We have all been subjected to high-stakes testing. And we can probably agree that there is an enormous degree of intimidation that comes along with these assessments. Intimidation causes anxiety. Anxiety can cause confusion. Confusion can cause poor test performance. Yikes! So if we perform poorly, we must be stupid! It is easy to fall into that perception or trap. Consider the high school student who fails the exit exam because of the math involved, and that math is deemed to be on the eighth-grade level of difficulty. Imagine how that sets the student up for the trap. Many students (and adults) who are adept at math but who have weak test-taking strategies are humiliated by these experiences. In reality, some may not have learned the content, or the test item did not reflect what or how they were taught, or they never learned the test-taking strategies that would allow them to show what they know.

Physical Fatigue and Stamina. Without sufficient warning or preparation, students will be unprepared for the intensity a testing situation delivers. Here, working with parents to be sure students get a good night's rest and eat nutritionally healthy food is critically important (see Chapter 9). In addition, practicing this intensity and rigor in the classroom, on occasion, may greatly help to get a feel for the real testing environment. Most students are used to taking tests of 45–55 minutes (or shorter) in length. They are not ready for the 180 minutes (or longer) test. It is a good idea to take full-length practice tests, if available, in weeks leading up to the test. Just like training for an athletic event, stamina and practice are critical.

Lack of Coping Strategies. Students often lack the personal coping strategies that would help them through stressful situations. Stress and anxiety have often been cited as one of the reasons why students with disabilities should be excluded from state and district assessments. But think about this as an adult. When you walk into a testing situation, why do you feel anxious? Are you unprepared for the test? Are you unfamiliar with the test format? Are you tired? Coping with potential stress during tests can be helped by teaching students how to think positively about their performance and visualize good test results.

Help students to identify ways in which to cope by teaching them how to get back to calm and productive states. One technique is for students to identify when their calm and productive state is disappearing. Teach them to know their signs and symptoms and when these symptoms begin to occur. Of course, there are different signs among students, but they are not hard to observe (e.g., nail biting, fatigue, changes in behavior). Relaxation techniques such as positive self-talk or affirmations are helpful, as are closing one's eyes and imagining oneself in a peaceful place.

Lack of Content Knowledge of the Curriculum Being Assessed. Not much to say here, except teach what is on the test to the best of your ability. Using the test specs or test matrices, usually available in test manuals, will enable you to be sure you have taught students the content and standards that will be assessed. Remember: Teaching to the test and teaching what is on the test are not the same. Whether it is a district-made criterion-referenced test (CRT) or a test publisher's norm-referenced test (NRT), knowing what is tested and how it is tested is a great starting point for preparing students for required assessments.

In summary, when preparing students for testing programs be sure to (1) review basic skills that will be tested (e.g., basic math concepts, grammar, punctuation, etc.); (2) teach and provide students practice on problem-solving skills; (3) teach students testing strategies that address the big picture of assessment (pacing, question selection, priority setting); (4) when possible, provide full-length practice tests to provide students with the opportunity to build stamina and familiarity while desensitizing them to the stress of a serious, often high-stakes testing environment; and (5) incorporate testing skills and strategies into daily instruction and classroom activity and assessment.

ASSESSMENT LITERACY

The term *assessment literacy* has been spurred by the tremendous vocabulary and methodology that has arisen around assessments, particularly district and state tests. While you do not need to become a psychometric expert to understand tests and help prepare students to improve their performance on these exams, you should have some knowledge of the basics of assessment terminology and philosophy. This knowledge will help you know what to emphasize and what to ignore as you help students improve their test performance.

Some basic terminology, which you may or may not already know, appears in Box 5.1. These are some of the terms that can be used to describe the tests that your students are required to take. As we use some of the terms of assessment in this chapter (and other chapters), you can refer back to these definitions.

Know the purpose of tests. Primary points to remember about district and state tests are that they might have either high-stakes consequences (those that have a significant impact) or low-stakes consequences (those that have relatively minimal impact), and the consequences might apply to either the student, the educational system (districts, schools, administrators, and staff), or both. Of course, the way in which you explain these concepts will vary with the age of the students with whom you are working. Nevertheless, even students in early elementary grades need some explanation of these concepts.

When discussing the purpose of district and state tests, the points that you cover should give answers to the "why" questions—questions that address why various purposes are important. In Box 5.2, we provide you with some general ideas for discussions of the "why" questions with elementary, intermediate-, middle-, and senior-high-level students. As you will note, regardless of the level, the gist and tone of the discussions should be matter-of-fact and nonthreatening.

Box 5.1

Selected Assessment Terminology and Definitions

Glossary of Commonly Used Terms

Alternate Assessment

Alternate assessment is a substitute approach used in gathering information about the performance and progress of students who do not participate in typical state assessments. Under the reauthorized Individuals With Disabilities Education Act (IDEA), alternate assessments are to be used to measure the performance of students who are unable to participate in the regular assessment system, even with accommodations, and are based on either grade-level achievement standards or alternate achievement standards. Pending regulations for NCLB, at the time this book was written, give states the option of alternate assessment based on modified achievement standards if specific conditions are met.

Assessment

Assessment is the process of collecting data for the purpose of making decisions about individuals, groups, or systems.

Criterion-Referenced Test

Criterion-referenced tests (CRTs) are measures used to examine student performance relative to state or district criteria or standards. Instead of comparing students' scores to a national normative standard, scores are interpreted in terms of various performance standards—usually set at the district or state level (e.g., mastery vs. nonmastery; low proficiency, moderate proficiency, and high proficiency within a particular subject area).

Norm-Referenced Test

Norm-referenced tests (NRTs) provide a comparison of individual performance to that of a state or national comparison (standardization) sample. An NRT measures the performance of a student against the performance of other individuals. Use of the norm sample enables raw scores to be converted to grade-equivalent scores, percentile scores, and standard scores.

Percentile Scores

Percentile scores give the percentage of people in the normative sample that scored at or below a student's score (e.g., a percentile rank of 80 means that 80% of the normative group earned a score at or below the student's score).

Performance Assessment

Performance assessment is a form of testing that requires the creation of an answer or a project, rather than the selection of an answer (as in many traditional multiple-choice tests). In many cases, such assessments are intended to represent or simulate real-life situations that require problem solving. The term is often used synonymously with authentic assessment.

(Continued)

(Continued)

Portfolio Assessment

Portfolio assessment is a collection of student-generated or student-focused products that provides the basis for judging student accomplishment. In school settings, portfolios might contain extended projects, drafts of student work, teacher comments and evaluations, assessment results, and self-evaluations. The products typically depict the range of skills of the student or reveal the improvement in a student's skill level over time.

Raw Scores

Raw scores are obtained when you sum the score on each item. If items are scored dichotomously (1 or 0), then a raw score represents the total number of items answered correctly.

Standards-Based Assessment

Standards-based assessment consists of an assessment instrument, battery, or system that has been constructed to measure the achievement of individual students or student populations in attaining certain standards, which are generally established by local districts or state educational agencies. Most state-level standards-based assessment programs that are currently in place measure student performance against articulated standards in core academic content areas, such as reading, mathematics, writing, science, and social studies.

Standard Scores

Standard scores are linear transformations of raw scores and are considered the easiest to interpret. With standard scores, the mean and standard deviation of any distribution can be placed onto a similar scale. A common example of standard scores is a typical intelligence quotient (IQ) test with a mean of 100 and a standard deviation of 15.

Reliability

Reliability is the extent to which a test measures what it purports to measure, time after time. Reliability also refers to the accuracy, precision, or stability of a measuring instrument.

Validity

Test validity, simply stated, refers to a test that measures what is says it measures.

SOURCE: The definitions in this paper were adapted from the definitions used by Drs. Elliott and Thurlow in their work at the National Center on Educational Outcomes.

Know the nature of the test. Students must be prepared for the test by having a sense of familiarity with the test, although they have never seen the test. To provide them with this sense of familiarity, you will need to know the test well. In other words, you need to know more than just the content area tested or that the test is norm referenced or criterion referenced.

Nearly every test developed today conforms to a test matrix that describes the types of items and nature of content that are included in the test. A couple

Box 5.2

Points to Make in Discussing the Purpose of State and District Assessments

Topic	Elementary (Grades 1–3)	Intermediate (Grades 4–5)	Middle (Grades 6–8)	Senior High (Grades 9–11)
School Consequences	This test is used to determine what you have been taught and will help us decide how our school is performing. You should do your best so that our school earns high marks.	This test is used to determine what you have been taught in this school. This test will help us determine whether this school has taught you what you need to know. You should do your best so that our school will earn high marks.	This test is used to measure what you know so that the state department of education (or the appropriate decision maker) can decide whether our school is doing what is necessary to educate you. You should do your best on this assessment so that our school will earn high marks.	This test is used to measure what you know so that the state department of education (or the appropriate decision maker) can decide whether to give our school extra funding. You should do your best on this assessment.
Student Consequences	This test is used to determine what you have been taught and will help us know that you have learned what you need to learn in this grade to be ready for the next grade. You should do your best.	This test is used to determine what you have been taught and is used to determine whether you have learned what you need to know to move to the next grade. You should do your best.	This test is used to measure what you know so that we can determine whether you have the skills needed to move to the next grade level (or to graduate from high school). You should do your best.	This test measures what you know so that the school board can verify that you have the skills necessary to move to the next grade level (or to graduate from high school). You should do your best.
School and Student Consequences	This test is used to determine what you have been taught and will help us decide how our school is doing. This test will also help us find out if you have learned what you need to know to be ready for the next grade. You should do your best.	This test is used to determine what you have been taught in this school and will assess whether this school has taught you what you need to know. The test is also used to determine whether you have learned what you need to know to move to the next grade level. You should do your best.	This test is used to measure what you know so that the state department of education (or the appropriate decision maker) can decide whether our school is doing what it needs to be doing to educate you. This test is also used to determine whether you have the skills that you need to move to the next grade (or to graduate from high school). You should do your best.	This test is used to measure what you know so that the state department of education (or the appropriate decision maker) can decide whether to give the school extra money. This test is also used to measure what you know so that the school board can verify that you have the skills that you need to move to the next grade (or to graduate from high school). You should do your best.

Box 5.3

Example of a Test Matrix for a Typical Standards-Based State Test

	Multiple Choice	Short Answer	Percentage of Test	Multiple-Choice Points	Short-Answer Points
Research	6	3	20	6	6
Geology	6	3	20	6	6
Biology	10	6	30	10	10
Physical Science	10	6	30	10	12

Mathematics Problem Solving Makeup of Test

SOURCE: This matrix was adapted from one level of a state test blueprint. The content areas and numbers have been changed for illustrative purposes.

Box 5.4

Example of a Test Matrix for a Typical Norm-Referenced Test

Mathematics Problem Solving Test Levels

	1	2	3	4	5	6	7	8	9	10	11	12	13
Whole number computation			X	X	X	X							
Number sense and numeration	X	X	X	X	X	X							
Geometry and spatial sense	X	X	X	X	X	X							
Measurement	X	X	X	X	X	X	X	X	X	X			
Statistics and probability	X	X	X	X	X	X							
Fractions and decimals			X	X	X	X							
Patterns and relationships	X	X	X	X	X	X							
Estimation					X	X	X	X	X	X			
Problem-solving strategies			X	X	X	X	X	X	X	X	X	X	X
Number and number relations							X	X	X	X			
Number systems and theory							X	X	X	X			
Patterns and functions							X	X	X	X			
Algebra							X	X	X	X	X	X	X
Statistics							X	X	X	X	X	X	X

	Mathematics Problem Solving Test Levels												
	1	2	3	4	5	6	7	8	9	10	11	12	13
Probability							X	X	X	X	X	X	X
Geometry							X	X	X	X			
Functions											X	X	X
Geometry—synthetic											X	X	X
Geometry—algebraic											X	X	X
Trigonometry											X	X	X
Discrete mathematics											X	X	X
Calculus concepts											X	X	X

of typical test matrices are presented in Boxes 5.3 and 5.4. Obtain one of these for the test for which you are preparing students. You should be able to get one from your district's research and evaluation division, the state department of education, or the test publisher. Often, the test matrix is provided in the test's manual. You will find it well worth your effort to obtain this matrix, because its contents can help provide the familiarity that is needed and guide practice sessions and worksheets that you will provide to your students. The percentage of time that you spend on different types of concepts, skills, and strategies can directly correspond to the percentage of these types of items that will appear on the test—if you have the test matrix to guide your preparation activities.

A test matrix can be further expanded to directly show the links to needed instruction. Long Beach Unified Schools performed this task for the formerly required state assessment—the Stanford 9. The district took the test matrix a step further (refer to the partial analysis in Box 5.5). By taking this action, teachers know not only what content is tested but also how it is tested, what specific types of items are used, and what prerequisite skills are needed.

Knowledge about the state and district tests and about the characteristics of students who have disabilities is now generating renewed interest in how to ensure that these tests accurately measure what students know and can do. For example, educators who are working with students who are blind and visually impaired have generated several principles that can guide the review and development of state and district tests for these students (Box 5.6).

SETTING GOALS, TARGETS, AND EXPECTATIONS

What feelings do you associate with assessment, especially high-stakes assessment? Eager anticipation, confidence, and well-being? Hardly. Most folks

Box 5.5

Partial Test Matrix Analysis*

Test Cluster	Number of Items and Sample Format	Content Domain	Tested Skills	Prerequisite Skills
Synonyms Recognize a synonym from a printed word	**18 items** A filly is a kind of • turtle • rabbit • horse • frog	Parts of speech, verbs, some nouns, some adjectives	1. To be able to discriminate between at least one close synonym and the precise definition. 2. To be able to discriminate between words that make sense in the sentence and the one that captures the same meaning.	• Ability to show conceptual understanding by discriminating between close approximations of meaning and precise meaning. • Be able to answer questions and give examples that are not just close enough but right on.
Multiple Meanings Use context to determine meaning of a known word with multiple meanings	**6 items** I cannot bear to tell my mom I skipped school. In which sentence does the word **bear** mean the same thing as in the sentence above? • I saw a bear eating my picnic lunch. • The bridge will bear 10 tons. • My brother bears well in school. • He bears up well under pressure	Words that change their meaning depending on what part of speech they are or depending on the context of a sentence; words can be one year below, at grade level, or one year above grade level.	1. Recognize that a word that is issued in a sentence (part of speech) can sometimes change its meaning. 2. Recognize homographs. 3. Recognize that context might change the meaning of a word.	• Understanding what context is. • Understanding that meaning resides in use, not just in the word itself. • Ability to write sentences using the same word to mean different things. • Awareness of spelling patterns and homographs.

Test Cluster	Number of Items and Sample Format	Content Domain	Tested Skills	Prerequisite Skills
Context Use context clues to assign the meaning to an unknown word	**6 items** Use the other words in the sentence to help you figure out what the underlined word means. After the earthquake, the dog dug through the *rubble* until he found his master. • yard • house • broken concrete • tunnel	Verbs, nouns, and adjectives that would not likely be encountered in third-grade literature but that could occur in upper-elementary grades.	1. Ability to get main ideas from sentences. 2. Ability to test hypotheses about language meaning and select best guesses.	• Ability to predict answers to questions without complete information. • Wide experience with a variety of above-grade level text that might be difficult but still comprehensive with guidance. • Large vocabulary • Word-attack skills (prefixes, root words, etc.)

* Prepared by the Long Beach Unified Public Schools for the Grade 3 Reading—Language Arts Stanford 9.

Box 5.6

Making Tests Accessible for Students With Visual Impairments: Considering the Unique Needs

Item Development and Review

1. Educators with specialization in the field of visual impairments must be included in the test item development process.

2. All test items must be reviewed by persons familiar with visual disability issues to ensure that no test item is biased or discriminatory toward persons with visual impairments.

3. It is recommended that as much information as possible be included in the text of a test item. This will help prevent the introduction of pictures that contain information necessary for selection of the correct answer, but which cannot be adequately brailled, presented in large print, or described in audio format.

4. In general, use of "vision specific" language can be maintained, e.g., "Look at the following list of animals."

5. The test item pool must be large enough for bias and item review committees to replace items determined to be inaccessible in braille, large print, or audio formats.

6. A representative sample of students with visual impairments needs to be included in any field-testing of the assessment, as prescribed in Standard 10.3 (p. 106) of the Standards for Educational and Psychological Testing (1999).

7. All practice materials must be provided in accessible format at the same time that print practice materials are provided. Allow sufficient time for accessible format preparation.

8. Provisions should be made to conduct item analyses for accessible format test items.

Large Print Formats and Graphics

Some students with visual impairments read regular print materials and enlarge the print by using optical devices. Others read large print materials. This section offers information regarding the development and implementation of assessments for students with visual impairments who require large print materials. Generally, two popular methods exist for enlarging tests. The regular print test can be enlarged through photocopying, or an electronic version of the test can be manipulated to reformat test items and enlarge or change the font as needed. The latter method is preferable unless issues outlined in this section have been addressed during the test development and the regular print test has been designed using universal design principles. Manipulating an electronic version of the test can best yield a large print version that incorporates the optimum reading mode for the student who uses large print.

Generally, reading skills that are difficult for a person with low vision who reads print include the following:

- Visual scanning and skimming of text
- Differentiating between subtle colors and patterns used in pictures or graphs
- Reading at a speed commensurate with regular print readers

- Shifting gaze from a picture or graph to test item and back again
- Shifting gaze from test booklet to answer sheet documents
- Capturing an entire picture
- Moving from one line of text to the next
- Interpreting pictures (particularly complex pictures)
- Reading for extended periods of time

Excerpts taken from Allman, C. (2004). Making tests accessible for students with visual impairments: A guide for test publishers, test developers, and state assessment personnel (2nd ed.). Louisville, KY: American Printing House for the Blind. Available from www.aph.org

experience feelings of anxiety, fear, and nervousness. Do we really get a valid measure of what students know and can do when they enter assessment environments with these feelings? In addition, sometimes the onslaught of these feelings is the result of expectations of others—in other words, what we expect, we get. If students perceive that they are not expected to do well on a classroom test or other assessment, then guess what usually happens? They don't do well. Remember the Hawthorne effect? Three groups of teachers were assigned three separate groups of students. One group was said to be very low achievers; the second, average achievers; and the third, high achievers. In reality, all the students were of average ability. The teachers worked with students, and at the end of the experiment, they were asked to rate and grade students on specific tasks. Guess how the groups performed? You guessed it—low, average, and above average, respectively. These types of effects are well documented in research, just as the placebo effect has been studied in medicine. A wise educator keeps these effects in mind. Researchers have found that simple statements can have significant influence on test performance of students.

Back to the feelings of anxiety and stress—the assessment experience does not need to be like this. As has been said many times, we need to shift or refocus our emphasis from assessment *of* learning to assessment *for* learning. One way to work toward this shift is to involve students in assessment for learning in the following ways.

Help students understand the learning targets they need to aim for. Students need to know what targets they are aiming for. Although they may not be the ones students necessarily desire, the targets they need are the ones that are necessary to be successful in today's accountability system of state and district assessment systems. Today, almost all tests that are used for accountability purposes are linked to some kind of proficiency level score, so that when reporting scores they can be meaningfully tied to concepts such as "basic," "proficient," and "advanced."

The first step to help students better define these levels is to help them understand, as appropriate, how many correct items are needed to be considered proficient. For example, 16 of the 30 items of the math subtest must be correct for a proficient score. This kind of information is particularly useful when a student must retake a test or subtest. Being able to define the number of additional correct items is often helpful and anxiety reducing to the student.

Ways to achieve this during classroom instruction can be to share not only learning standards and proficiency levels but also the rubrics or performance standards on which these levels are attained. Stating targets in student-friendly ways is important. Showing them learning rubrics and scoring guides helps. To do this, teachers themselves must be knowledgeable about these requirements.

When the purpose of the test is school accountability—with consequences assigned to schools, staff, and administrators—the motivation for doing one's best might be lacking. One way to accomplish this goal is to give students a practice test that you score. Setting a slightly higher level of performance as a goal to achieve with the student is one way to increase motivation for doing one's best on the test. You can also link this performance to class grades or student rewards to increase motivation.

Teach students about self-assessment. When students understand and recognize the learning targets or standards, they will be better equipped to begin the process of self-assessment. Knowing how they performed in the past (or how they are performing now) can help identify realistic goals. Past classroom, district, or state assessment performance should be directly tied to each student goal setting based on this self-assessment. We can then teach the students how to self-assess their progress in relation to these targets. (See Chapter 3 for more information on data-based targets.)

Help students examine their own improvement with respect to the standards or learning targets. Collecting student work samples and having students analyze them over time helps students anchor themselves in expected levels of performance. Some teachers give students examples of exemplary and nonexemplary work and ask them to assess the work as if they were the final judge or scorer.

Make sure students know how to use their needed accommodations. Many students with disabilities may have classroom and assessment accommodations indicated in their Individualized Education Programs (IEPs). The first place these accommodations should show up is in classroom instruction. Two important aspects of accommodations, especially as students get older, are to make sure that they know why they need the accommodations and that they are not embarrassed to use them. Often students who need accommodations opt out of using them simply because they do not understand their importance. And, even more tragic, they have not been provided the opportunity to use them or apply them during classroom instruction, much less classroom assessments. It is important to help students realize that how they perceive the use of their needed accommodations may be different from how their classmates perceive their use. Student surveys have revealed that classmates of students with disabilities are supportive of the use of accommodations. Concerns arise about fairness only when students with disabilities are held to different standards for the same grades (e.g., having to get fewer items correct).

Provide students with the opportunity to articulate their understanding of the process toward the targets. Student-teacher and student-student learning conferences or activities provide students with the opportunity to express their understanding of the process of self-assessment or progress toward the standards or learning targets.

Empower students to set personal goals and next steps. Involving students in the process of assessing their learning provides students with an overall feeling of control over their path to learning and success. Studies have shown that this *control* has been conducive to producing learning results that are higher, as well as having a positive effect on student motivation. Let us be clear that it is not as easy as saying to students, "You are now in control of your learning destiny." We have to teach students the strategies and provide them with the learning experiences to get there.

In summary, we need to create learning environments that allow for valid assessment *for* learning. Educators can do this by encouraging rather than discouraging, building confidence rather than anxiety, bringing hope rather than hopelessness, offering success rather than frustration, and triggering smiles rather than tears.

PREPARING DAILY FOR THE TEST

Although better understanding the test and its requirements and setting goals are both important steps in preparing for the test, they are not the bulk of the activities that need to be undertaken to be sure that students are prepared for the test. Good instruction and varied methods and formats are essential ways you can use to prepare students daily, for assessment—*any* assessment. Here a few suggestions:

Review General Test Vocabulary Terms

Few of the more recent resources on test taking refer to test vocabulary as an essential part of preparing to take tests. Yet, there are key words that are used in tests, and it is usually dangerous to assume that students know what these words mean in the testing situation. You should make sure that they do know these words. Words and phrases such as *contrast*, *most accurate*, and a host of others often have special meaning in testing situations. Several of the key words to include in a review of test vocabulary terms are included in Box 5.7.

Review Specific Content-Area Terms

Although teaching the vocabulary of a content area is a natural part of instruction, you should review key terms prior to taking tests in the content area. Having a broad and well-established vocabulary is clearly an advantage when taking tests. This is the reason why almost every test-preparation course or text emphasizes the need to stress vocabulary. The fact that a student might receive an accommodation (such as having someone read the test or clarify the test directions) does not negate the need for ensuring that students know the content-area terms.

Box 5.7			
Common Test Vocabulary Terms			
Analyze	Estimate	List	Pattern
Best	Evaluate	Most accurate	Point of view
Categorize	Explain	Most appropriate	Predict
Classify	Fact	Not	Reasonable
Compare	Group	Not like	Sequence
Conclude	Identify	Only one	Summarize
Contrast	Justify	Opinion	Transform
Describe	Least true	Order	Verify
Discuss	Like	Outline	

The best way to ensure that students have a broad vocabulary, of course, is to have them read frequently, to read to them often, and to make sure that they know the words that they are reading or hearing. Likewise, it is important to include in every lesson some time to ensure that the vocabulary in the lesson is understood. Making vocabulary a part of everything in and out of the classroom is helpful. For example, if students are learning spelling, they should learn not only to combine the letters in order to get the word but also to define what the word means and show how to use the word in a sentence.

Address the Administration of Tests

It is important to discuss with students the importance of test taking. The seriousness with which students approach classroom tests and district or state assessments should be the same. However, the reality is that when students take district or state tests, especially high-stakes tests, the tests themselves are handled differently from the way in which most classroom tests are handled. The more aware the students are of these special administration procedures, the less likely the procedures themselves are to create stress and anxiety for the student who is taking the test. Overtly discussing these procedures and letting students experience them can go a long way toward improving test scores. At the same time, these procedures familiarize students with what is going to happen in any special situation and help them prepare for these unique situations.

Some of the specific administration procedures that might be encountered in testing situations include bubbling in, stopping at certain points, not turning pages, and knowing whether to work fast or methodically. Many other administration procedures exist that might be unique to the test that your students take. Whenever possible, incorporate these procedures into your classroom assessments.

Provide General Strategies for Different Types of Items

Although some state and district tests might use performance items or even portfolios, the most common types of items are those with which we are all familiar: true/false, multiple choice, fill in the blank, short answer, and essay. These types of questions have been and continue to be the substance of testing, including classroom testing, although the amount of emphasis given to each type ebbs and flows with changes in perceptions about what learning should be like and what particular types of items really test.

You should not plan to expose students to information about types of test items that they might never see on a real test. Using your knowledge about the makeup of your state or district test (from the test matrix), you should provide students with instruction on approaches for various item types. The kinds of information that you might want to provide to students are shown in Box 5.8. Remember, however, that the type of item in a test should not completely determine the focus of instruction. Some evidence exists that students who prepare for essay tests, regardless of the type of test administered, do better than students who prepare for the specific type of item in a test. Similar information exists that can assist students with preparing for tests in specific content areas. In their text, *Teaching Test-Taking Skills: Helping Students Show What They Know*, Scruggs and Mastropieri (1992) provide excellent examples of these types of strategies.

Create Similar Test Formats

Although the adage "practice makes perfect" might be carrying things too far, practice is important when it comes to taking tests. The more familiar students are with the format, procedures, and mechanics of testing, the more likely they are to perform better—even if nothing different has been done to the instruction that they receive.

Develop your own practice items that are similar to those items in the tests. Model your classroom assessment items according to those your students will be required to take on state or district assessments. Depending on the ages of your students, you might even have them attempt to develop items of each type that they will be taking. By performing this task, the students begin to understand how tests relate to the content of a topic—thereby making it easier for them to study the "right stuff" in preparation for a test.

Give the Student One or More Test-Taking Strategies

Today, there are many test-taking strategies available in books, journals, and even the Internet. The teaching of such strategies almost always has been proven worthwhile. For example, a strategy developed just for test taking is called SCORER:

S—Schedule your time

C—Clue words

O—Omit difficult questions

R—Read carefully

E—Estimate your answer

R—Review

Box 5.8

Suggestions for Answering Different Types of Questions

Item Type	Suggestions for Students
True/False	Do not be concerned with expected patterns of responses (e.g., do not try to make the number of true responses and the number of false responses equal).
	Watch out for absolute statements—ones that contain words such as "never" or "always"—and realize that these are almost never true (but they can be true sometimes).
Multiple choice	Treat each answer option as a true/false statement (i.e., determine whether each option is true or false), then respond to the stem demands.
	Mark out absurd items so that you are only choosing among the more likely options.
	Proceed through items relatively quickly, going with your first guess, and changing later only if you are certain of a different response.
Fill in the blank	Make a best guess based on content knowledge, but look for cues in the structure of the sentence.
	Be sure that the word(s) you choose fits the grammatical structure of the item.
Short answer	Recognize short-answer questions as such, and do not write too much.
	Respond directly to the point of the question; help yourself to perform this task by underlining the key elements requested.
Essay	Write enough to be convincing.
	Keep your answer organized. To achieve this goal, take notes beside the item or jot notes onto a separate piece of paper.
	Be neat.
	Use strategies to help guide the writing process (e.g., SNOW—study the question; note the important points; organize your thoughts; write to the question; Scruggs & Mastropieri, 1992).

This strategy was developed by Ritter and Idol-Maestas (1986) and is explained nicely in the book, *Tools for Learning: A Guide to Teaching Study Skills*, by Gall, Gall, Jacobsen, and Bullock (1990). Students using strategies such as SCORER have a systematic and stable way to approach tests. This feeling of control over what they must do goes a long way toward bolstering the confidence with which students with face tests—particularly, students who have disabilities.

A variety of mini-strategies can also be useful. These strategies are found scattered throughout various sources and range from simplistic advice such as

> **Box 5.9**
>
> **Self-Regulation and Time Management**
>
> **Recommendations for Self-Regulation and Time-Management Strategies**
>
> Be wise in the use of time. Use strategies that help you go through certain steps, rather than getting bogged down by specific items.
>
> Practice monitoring your own time on-task. Perhaps start by having an alarm clock set at intervals of five minutes. Each time the clock rings, mark on a log whether you are on task. Hone your on-task skills to the point that you can maintain on-task behavior for the entire duration of a test. If the inability to do so is related to your disability, explore accommodations that might help your on-task behavior.
>
> Have everything that you need at your fingertips so that no unnecessary time is spent looking for or retrieving needed items (e.g., erasers, spare pencils, tissues, etc.).
>
> During practice tests, figure out good pacing strategies for you to be able to complete the test in a reasonable amount of time.

"read the test directions carefully" to tricks such as "answer the easy questions first." Many of these mini-strategies are picked up by good students on their own. Other students, particularly students who have disabilities, typically do not pick up such strategies. Therefore, the strategies need to be taught to these students. Not doing so provides other students with an unfair advantage.

Most learning strategies have been developed for instruction rather than testing. Yet, many of the learning strategies could be adapted to apply these strategies to testing situations, depending on the needs of individual students (Box 5.9).

HELPING STUDENTS BECOME ADVOCATES FOR THEIR OWN TESTING NEEDS

Students must become advocates for their own testing needs, especially as they become older. This skill is critical for them to have as they make the transition to high school, postsecondary education, and later into the work world. Being able to ask for what is needed is not the only necessary skill. Of course, this skill is the most critical. But beyond that, the student should know how and when to ask for accommodations in the most appropriate manner possible. This action involves developing interpersonal skills that some students lack. These skills should be a focus of instruction, because ideally they are among the IEP goals that are set for students who lack appropriate skills when advocating for themselves.

For school-aged students, Box 5.10 provides a General Education Profile that highlights the important aspects, especially needed accommodations, for classroom instruction and testing. One of the most critical aspects of teaching students with disabilities is that all teachers who teach them specifically must

Box 5.10

IEP Summary for General Educators

Distributed to: _____

_____

_____

Date: _____ / _____ / _____

RSP Teacher: _____

Room #: _____

Ext. _____

Conference Period: _____

School Site _____

Student Name: _____ Grade _____ ELL Level _____

Most Recent IEP date ___ / ___ / ___ Next IEP Due ___ / ___ / ___ ☐ **Behavior Plan:** The student has an IEP Behavior Plan (see attached).

Disability Area: _____ **Learning Disability** _____ **Emotional Disability** _____ **Autism** _____ **Other** _____

The student has the following specific area of strengths and needs:

Specific Areas of Need   *Specific Strengths*

_____ math calculation _____

_____ math reasoning _____

_____ reading comprehension _____

_____ basic reading skills _____

_____ written expression _____

_____ listening comprehension _____

_____ oral expression _____

The area(s) of need is due to a deficit in

_____ attention   _____ visual processing   _____ auditory processing

_____ sensory motor skills   _____ conceptualization   _____ expression

and is not primarily the result of environmental, cultural, economic disadvantage, or limited English proficiency.

Relevant medical information: _____

Current reading level: _____   ☐ **Enrolled in a reading intervention class** _____

                                            Specify

Learns best when _____

_____

_____

IEP Goals:

Content Area/Std #	Summary of Goal		How to Evaluate

(Continued)

(Continued)

Instructional/Assessment Accommodations

☐ The student has accommodations and modifications; please see attached IEP pages.

- All instructional and assessment accommodations should be given to the student during the class/subject indicated.
- The RSP teacher should indicate the accommodations that each specific student requires per the IEP by checking the coordination box.
- If a box is checked, the general education teacher should review the attached accommodations IEP pages.

Subject	Setting	Time	Scheduling	Presentation	Read Aloud	Calculator	Other:	Other:
Sample: *Math*	✓	✓				✓		

For further information and to review the entire IEP, please see the student's cumulative file.

know their strengths, needs, and accommodations. The profile in Box 5.10 is one example of how this information can be shared.

SUMMARY

In this chapter, we gave you lots of ideas about preparing students for testing. We covered the need for you and your students to understand the basics of assessment—its purpose and the nature of tests that students will take. Setting performance goals and placing test taking within a reasonable set of expectations fits in the larger scheme of preparing for test taking. The array of ways to prepare students for tests, beyond the prerequisite good instruction, are ones that you can use and expand on as you see their benefits for improving the performance of students.

Remember, we can proactively prepare students to take tests. So, think about doing the following:

- First and foremost, teach what is on the test! Provide students the opportunity to learn the content matter that will be assessed.
- Incorporate test preparation as a regular routine into your classroom instruction and testing.
- Use a variety of test item formats on your classroom tests. Doing this provides students with the opportunity to become familiar with item formats that they will be confronted with come testing time.
- Capitalize and teach thinking skills. Many of the assessments administered today tap into students' critical-thinking skills. Instead of taking any old answer, including the correct one, from a student, use the HDYKT tactic—How Do You Know That? Students then have to explain how they arrived at the answer. You will be amazed at what you discover about their thinking processes.
- Talk to students about the reason for classroom assessments and the importance of their doing their best. Then extrapolate that into a discussion on the reason and importance of state assessments.
- Make sure students' IEPs reflect needed accommodations and that those accommodations are used regularly during classroom instruction, tests, and district and state assessments.
- Teach students to become their own advocates for their testing needs. Be sure they know and can use their needed accommodations and feel comfortable asking for them when they are not offered.

TEST YOUR KNOWLEDGE

Complete the following fill-in-the-blank statements. Reread parts of this chapter if the words that go in the blanks are not obvious to you.

1. Although you do not need to become a psychometric expert to help students improve their test scores, it is important to have basic assessment _____.

2. To help you and your students understand the nature of a district or state test, you should get a test _____ to help with planning and preparation.

3. _____ can have a significant effect on how students perform on a test, although they are not directly related to the test's content or to the student's skills.

4. Before testing, the student's _____ should be reviewed for information about accommodations.

5. Having a broad and well-established _____ is an advantage for students when taking tests.

6. In addition to obtaining practice items from your district or state assessment office, you can _____ some of your own items for students to take.

7. Treating each answer option as a true or false item is a strategy for taking _____ items.

8. Time management and self-_____ are related strategies that are frequently mentioned in test-preparation books.

9. It is a good idea to model your classroom _____ items according to those that students will be required to take on district or state assessments.

10. Students must become _____ for their own testing needs.

ANSWERS

1. literacy (p. 76)

2. matrix (p. 78)

3. Expectations (p. 85)

4. IEP (p. 86)

5. vocabulary (p. 87)

6. develop (p. 89)

7. multiple choice (p. 90)

8. regulation (p. 91)

9. assessment or test (p. 91)

10. advocates (p. 91)

REFLECTIONS ON CHANGE

See Appendix A for the Reflections on Change activity for this chapter (191).

RECOMMENDED RESOURCES

Abbamont, G., & Brescher, A. (1997). *Test smart: Ready to use test-taking strategies and activities for grades 5–12.* Upper Saddle River, NJ: Prentice-Hall.

Allman, C. (2004). *Making tests accessible for students with visual impairments: A guide for test publishers, and state assessment personnel. (2nd ed.).* Louisville, KY: American Printing House for the Blind.

Bigge, J. L., & Stump, C. S. (1999). *Curriculum, assessment, and instruction for students with disabilities.* Belmont, CA: Wadsworth.

Arter, J. A. (2004). Assessment for learning: Classroom assessment to improve student achievement and well-being. In J. E. Wall & G. R. Waltz (Eds.), *Measuring up: Assessment issues for teachers, counselors, and administrators* (pp. 463–484). Greensboro, NC: CAPS Press.

Eaton, H. (1996). *Self-advocacy: How students with learning disabilities can make the transition from high school to college.* Santa Barbara, CA: Excel.

Fry, R. (1996). *Ace any test.* Franklin Lakes, NJ: Career Press.

Gall, M. D., Gall, J. P., Jacobsen, D. R., & Bullock, T. L. (1990). *Tools for learning: A guide to teaching study skills.* Alexandria, VA: Association for Supervision and Curriculum Development.

Gamsby, L. H. (1987). *Coping with school: Organizational and learning techniques for parents, teachers, & students.* Concord, NH: Parent Information Center.

Gilbert, S. D. (1998). *How to do your best on tests.* New York: Beech Tree Books.

Klingner, J. K., & Vaughn, S. (1999). Students' perceptions of instruction in inclusion classrooms: Implications for students with learning disabilities. *Exceptional Children, 66*(1), 23–37.

Polloway, E. A., Bursuck, W. D., Jyanthi, M., Epstein, M. H., & Nelson, J. A. (1996). Treatment acceptability: Determining appropriate interventions within inclusive classrooms. *Intervention in School and Clinic, 31*(3), 133–144.

Pressley, M., & Woloshyn, V. (1995). *Cognitive strategy instruction that really improves children's academic performance (2nd ed.).* Cambridge, MA: Brookline Books.

Ritter, S., & Idol-Maestas, L. (1986). Teaching middle school students to use a test-taking strategy. *Journal of Educational Research, 79*(6), 350–357.

Rubenstein, J. (2004). Test preparation: What makes it effective? In J. E. Wall & G. R. Waltz (Eds.), *Measuring up: Assessment issues for teachers, counselor, and administrators* (pp. 397–416). Greensboro, NC: CAPS Press.

Scruggs, T. E. & Mastropieri, M. A. (1992). *Teaching test-taking skills: Helping students show what they know.* Cambridge, MA: Brookline Books.

INTERNET RESOURCES

Access Center: www.K8accesscenter.org
American Printing House for the Blind: www.aph.org/
Council for Exceptional Children: www.cec.sped.org/
Educational Testing Service: www.ets.org/
National Association of Test Developers: www.natd.org/
Scholastic Testing Systems: www.testprep.com/

Addressing the Needs of IEP/ELLs

Excellence is never an accident.

—Anonymous

We are now at a point where we must educate our children in what no one knew yesterday, and prepare our schools for what no one knows yet.

—Margaret Mead

Everything we have talked about so far applies to *all* students with disabilities. But sometimes it is necessary to clarify that this *all* really includes those students who are learning English. These students have been given a number of labels in educational systems across the country. Most recently, we use the term *English language learners*, or ELLs, to refer to students who are learning English while in schools in the United States. The official term that is used in federal law to refer to these students is "limited English proficient," so we have sometimes referred to them as students with *limited English proficiency*, or LEP, students. For shorthand here, we are referring to students who have a disability and who are also English language learners as IEP/ELLs. Our intent in using this shortcut terminology is only to make it easier for you to read this chapter.

There are many concerns about whether we can accurately diagnose disabilities in ELLs, and these concerns are very real and complicated. As you might guess, the difficulty is not so much in identifying students who have physical disabilities or significant cognitive disabilities. The difficulties arise most often related to disabilities that are not outwardly evident, such as learning disabilities, emotional disabilities, and even sensory disabilities. We are not going to solve those issues in this chapter. What we are going to attempt to do is ensure that you know that not only are IEP/ELLs to be included in state and district assessments, but also that we need to make sure that these students have the opportunity to perform their best on the assessments. There are many things that can be done to make sure this happens.

In this chapter we intend to give you some tools for working with these students. First, we describe a little bit about who these students are, how many there are, and some of their characteristics. Then we address several key issues for improving the achievement and test performance of these students: how to make decisions about their participation in assessments, what accommodations they may need, and what we know about their performance on state assessments. We also address the instructional issues that are created by students who are learning English, and we examine the standards-based instructional strategies that have been recommended for IEP/ELLs.

It will become obvious to you that we do not have all the answers when it comes to IEP/ELLs, but we do have some starting steps for you to take.

WHO ARE IEP/ELLs?

Let's start with some terminology. We used the term *English language learners* (ELLs) because it is used widely today for students who are in the process of learning English and whose English skills are limited. The most common terms are probably ELL and LEP, but many additional terms are used in schools, districts, and states today. Some of the more common ones and the fine distinctions among them are provided in Box 6.1. As you will note in this list of words, some terms might be used interchangeably, such as ELLs and LEP students because they generally refer to the same group of students. Other terms have very different meanings, and they may be misused by those who really don't understand the differences among the groups. A common mistake is to equate students whose home language is other than English, commonly referred to as having a non-English-language background (NELB), and LEP students.

A complication related to terminology is that the same student may be considered to be an English learner for some purposes but not for others. For example, a student may not count as an English learner when the school decides whether he or she is eligible for ESL (English as a second language) or bilingual educational services. But the same student may count as an English learner when he or she participates in an assessment.

Box 6.1

Clarification of Terminology

Term	Definition	Equivalent Terms	Nonequivalent Terms
Bilingual student	Student who speaks two languages; one of the languages may be English.		Limited English proficiency (LEP) student
Bilingual education student	Student in the process of learning English and at the same time content in his or her first language.		ESL student
English language learner (ELL)	Student in the process of learning English, either oral or written.	LEP student, LM student	ESL student, bilingual ed. student
English as a second language (ESL) student	Student learning English through English as a second language class.		Bilingual ed. student
Language minority (LM) student	Student whose first language is in the minority in the educational setting where he or she is located.	LEP student, ELL	ESL student, bilingual ed. student
Non-English-language background (NELB)	Student whose home language is other than English, regardless of whether the student is fully English proficient.	LEP student, ELL, LM student	
Second language learner	An individual learning a second language; the first language may or may not be English.		ELL, LEP student

How Many Are There?

English language learners with disabilities in the United States make up about 9.2% of all students who are ELLs, according to a study conducted in 2001–2002. Since this finding was made public, conversations have occurred about whether this percentage might be an underestimate of the "true" population of these students, given educator and psychologist concerns about not being able to correctly identify disabilities when limited English skills make measurement of students' abilities, knowledge, and skills difficult.

Box 6.2

Percentages of All IEP Students and IEP/ELLs by Category

Disability	Percentage of All Students	Percentage of LEP Students
Specific learning disabilities	6.64%	5.16%
Speech/language impairments	2.72	2.17
Mental retardation	1.20	0.72
Emotional disturbance	1.00	0.23
Other health impairments	0.73	0.20
Developmental delay	0.32	0.15
Autism	0.26	0.12
Multiple disabilities	0.25	0.10
Hearing disabilities	0.18	0.16
Orthopedic impairments	0.16	0.14
Visual impairments	0.06	0.05
Traumatic brain injury	0.04	0.02
Deaf/blindness	0.01	0.005

The number of respondents who provided data on this item was from 518 to 534. The item response represented 84.8% to 90.1% of the weighted cases on this form. The responses were weighted at the form level to be nationally representative.

SOURCE: Data reprinted with permission from Table 2.3, "Percentages of All Students and LEP Students With Specific Disability Classifications" (District Special Education Services Questionnaire). In A. Zehler, H. J. Fleischman, P. J. Hopstock, M. L. Pendzick, & T. G. Stephenson. (2003). *Descriptive study of services to LEP students and LEP students with disabilities*, Special Topic Report #4: Findings on Special Education LEP Students (p. 8). Arlington, VA: Development Associates, Inc.

The population of ELLs has grown dramatically in the United States during the past 10 years, much more rapidly than the total student population. And although ELLs most often live in California, Texas, and Florida, these students are spread across the United States and indeed have an impact on nearly every school district.

What Are Their Characteristics?

Overall, IEP/ELLs reflect the characteristics of IEP students and the characteristics of ELLs. That is, most of these students have learning disabilities, followed by speech or language impairments (Box 6.2). Like the overall ELL population, they tend to be Spanish speaking. According to the nationally representative study conducted in 2001–2002 (in this chapter's Recommended Resources), three language groups had higher representation in the special education population than in the ELL population—Spanish language, Navajo language, and Lao language. Because ELLs have different language backgrounds, associated differences exist in their educational histories. These students may or may not have been born in the United States. They may or may not have come from a country with an educational system. They may or may not have participated in the educational system if one existed. They may have been in their home country's educational system for 10, 5, or 1 year (and all the variations in between) before coming to the United States. Not only are the educational systems varied, but other experiential factors may vary as well, and the amount of time that the student has been in them varies. For example, many students in the United States who arrived from war-torn countries may have spent considerable time in hiding or in refugee camps. All of these kinds of educational and experiential differences are intertwined with the language complexities that these students carry with them.

One more set of characteristics is important to understand. What is instruction like for these students—across the nation and, more important, in your district and your school? Students who receive instruction in U.S. schools typically receive their content instruction in English, perhaps supported by something in their first language. It is commonly accepted that students learning English first learn social English; that is, they learn to communicate with their peers and perhaps their teacher about social topics. Learning social English typically (complicated by all the other factors mentioned earlier) takes three to five years. Social English is not the same as academic English, the language of instruction. Academic English may take 7 to 10 years to master, yet it is the language in which most students receive instruction. Therefore, providing a translated version of an assessment may not be the best solution, because the student has not learned the content in his or her first language.

The differences between social and academic languages have been studied extensively by language-learning theorists. Common terms in this field are basic interpersonal communication skills (BICS) and cognitive academic language proficiency (CALP). It is generally accepted that students must reach a threshold of BICS before CALP can develop. In addition, however, the development of CALP is dependent on academic reasoning skills, which are more likely to exist or developed more quickly if the student has strong language skills in his or her first language, which in turn is facilitated by coming from a literate home background. To further complicate the issues, certain content areas may require a longer time for CALP to develop than others. For example, reading, social studies, and science are generally considered to require more time for CALP to develop; math and language require less time.

From the 2001–2002 study of IEP/ELLs across the nation, we learned that IEP/ELLs were less likely to receive extensive services for students with limited English proficiency than were ELLs not receiving special education services. They were also more likely to receive their instruction all in English and less likely to receive some use of native language than were ELLs who were not receiving special education services.

Language issues and special education services issues complicate making good decisions about instruction, accommodations that are needed, and how to improve achievement and test scores when students are taking state and district assessments. Wow—lots of areas to address!

Which Comes First: IEP or ELL?

This question may be unanswerable. In terms of legal rights, if a student has an IEP, all the rights that are connected to that IEP are held by the student. Yet all the issues and difficulties created by the fact that the student is learning English also apply. Instructionally, both disability and language needs must be addressed simultaneously. This is the only way in which performance on assessments (and, indeed, benefiting from instruction) can occur.

When most people ask questions about what comes first, they most often are really asking about who is responsible for the dollars required to meet the student's needs. This is especially true if special accommodations are needed either for instruction or for assessment. What we know is that this type of question does little to help the student. It is likely that an integration of dollars and services is needed, so that the needs of all are met equally.

We suggest that the question of "what comes first" is a nonquestion. Even if we could come up with an answer, it would be of little benefit to the student or to anyone else in the system.

PARTICIPATION OF IEP/ELLs IN DISTRICT AND STATE ASSESSMENTS

The participation of ELLs in state assessments is now specifically covered by federal law, the Elementary and Secondary Education Act (ESEA), more commonly known today as No Child Left Behind (NCLB). English language learners (or, according to federal terminology, LEP students) constitute one of the subgroups—just as students with disabilities are another subgroup.

No Child Left Behind has clarified the requirements for the participation of ELLs in state assessments and in NCLB's adequate yearly progress (AYP) accountability system. It has even introduced a measure of flexibility for this subgroup—allowing these students to be counted for up to three years after they have stopped receiving services for their English learning needs (in other words, after they technically no longer belong to the subgroup). States successfully argued that if students were dropped from the subgroup as soon as they were successful, the subgroup would never show improvement. Other areas of flexibility relate to the accountability and assessment requirements of NCLB. For example, a student who has been in the country less than one year does not need to be included in the reading accountability calculations. In fact, the student may not have to participate in the assessment, if the school decides that the student in not able to meaningfully participate in the assessment.

Although these nuances are interesting, when it comes to IEP/ELLs, the IEP requirements take precedence. Thus, these students are required to participate in all assessments—district and state—based on the requirements of the Individuals With Disabilities Education Act of 1997 (IDEA 97) and the Individuals With Disabilities Education Improvement Act of 2004 (IDEA 2004).

Given the complexity of figuring this out, it would be reasonable to expect that states would have developed rules, or at least guidelines, to clarify their assessment participation requirements for these students. Yet, a study conducted in 2003 revealed that only one state had a separate assessment policy that specifically addressed the participation of IEP/ELLs in state assessments. A couple of states did mention IEP/ELLs in their special education policy, and a few others mentioned them in their ELL policy.

Thus, looking at state policies gives us little guidance for how things should be for IEP/ELLs. We believe that if a student has a disability, that student should participate in the general assessment or alternate assessment under the same guidelines as other students with disabilities. The caveat is that the assessment should occur in the language of instruction or, even better, in the student's language of choice. We use the term "language of choice" to avoid the confusion of social language versus academic language and all the other complications of educational and experiential background. The IEP team should take into consideration the language characteristics of the LEP/ELL.

Of course, things are not always ideal, and language of choice may not always be a viable option. Certain tests, such as English tests, preclude allowing the student to use his or her language of choice. Similarly, many states insist that the student demonstrate English skills in all content areas to earn a high school diploma. These situations make it much more difficult to develop and implement what might be considered "best practice" in the assessment of IEP/ELLs.

It is also important to think about the goals of the students' instruction. These goals should include both academic content and the learning of the English language.

No Child Left Behind requires the administration of English proficiency tests to all LEP students. Thus, IEP/ELLs are to be included in this requirement as well. Typically, states have thought about accommodations and alternate assessments for their general content assessments, but not for their tests of English proficiency. They will need to expand their thinking for these assessments as well!

ACCOMMODATIONS

Accommodations are often needed for IEP/ELLs in order to address their needs related to both their disabilities and the fact that they are learning English. You may wonder whether the accommodations needed would be the same. It seems logical that these students may need extra time and maybe a separate setting. But are there some accommodations that might be needed for their language concerns and others for their disability concerns?

Because we are dealing with humans, whose needs aren't nicely separated between those related to disabilities and those related to language, it is probably not beneficial to analyze a student's needs separately. Instructionally, this kind of division makes little sense, but lists of accommodations that are allowed for assessments may or may not be separated for students with disabilities or students with LEP. Sometimes when the listed accommodations are divided, they just say the same things but have different labels. More often now, the lists are divided and different kinds of accommodations are included in each list.

> **Box 6.3**
>
> ## Examples of Linguistic Accommodations
>
> - Simplified English
> - Written native language translation of English test items
> - Native language test version
> - Oral interpretation of test items in the native language
> - Bilingual dictionary or glossary
> - Student response in native language
>
> Based on analysis of state assessment accommodation policies by Rivera, Collum, Shafer, and Sia (2004).

If this is the case, you will need to have both lists at hand, and you will need to justify the accommodations needed from each list.

A study of states' accommodation guidelines in 2003 indicated that four states specifically referred to IEP/ELLs. None of the states provided guidance to assist in the process of making decisions about which accommodations to select for students who both had a disability and were learning English. Box 6.3 expands on the accommodations provided in Box 4.1, some of which are appropriate only for students with disabilities, and some of which were appropriate for both IEP students and ELLs. In Box 6.3, those accommodations that are linguistic in nature are identified—these are ones that are designed to meet the language needs of ELLs.

Making decisions about accommodations for IEP/ELL students should follow the same basic procedures as decisions about accommodations for any student. They should be related to what happens in instruction, and they should meet the specific needs of the student. Setting up a questionnaire that gets at needs (like that in Chapter 4) works for IEP/ELLs.

ASSESSMENT PERFORMANCE

Federal law does not require that states or districts disaggregate the scores of IEP/ELLs. Yet, there are reasons to do so, particularly if there is interest in ensuring that these students are making the improvements in achievement and assessment performance that they should be. It is always better to know how they are doing than not to know. And insight can be gained by looking at the group of students who are IEP/ELLs.

Few states currently look separately at the test performance of their IEP/ELLs, and those that do are not necessarily the ones that you might expect. Studies conducted by Thurlow, Albus, Shyyan, Liu, and Barrera (2004) showed that only one state had a policy on its books that required the reporting of assessment results for IEP/ELLs. Six states actually reported IEP/ELL assessment results for at least one general assessment administered in 2002–2003 (interestingly, not the state that had IEP/ELL assessment policies); two states reported information for IEP/ELLs on the state's special education alternate assessment; and two states reported information for IEP/ELLs on the state's language proficiency assessment. Only two of the states in this list of six states are on the list of states with the largest ELL populations in terms of number or density. The message is that it takes interest in what is happening to these students—and that interest can come from anywhere. If your state or district is not providing a picture of how these students are doing for you, then you need to dig into the data yourself (see Chapter 3).

The studies that have been conducted to look at what we know about the performance of IEP/ELLs indicate that their performance is not very good. Generally, it is below the performance of either IEP students or ELLs as a group. There are probably many reasons for this finding. But there are also some surprising findings in these data—and they should give us pause. For example, in one study in the early 2000s (and at this point, there had been only one study), the lowest performing category was IEP/ELLs with learning disabilities. Isn't that surprising? Wouldn't one expect that it might be students with mental retardation or perhaps some other category? Is there something about expectations for these students that is affecting instruction for them? Another unexpected finding was that students with low performance on language proficiency measures performed unexpectedly high on a graduation examination. In fact, on one language proficiency measure, it was suggested that students not be exposed to other measures if low performance was obtained on that part of the assessment. Yet, students in fact passed a graduation exam on the skills that they would not have been assessed on according to the instructions on the one measure. Perhaps we are making too many assumptions and being guided by too many old and low expectations. We need to throw these away!

Discussions about what to do assessment-wise for IEP/ELLs have been initiated. Suggestions made by the National Research Council in *Testing, Teaching, and Learning* (Box 6.4) are a first step in thinking about ELLs in assessments. For example, exposing students to assessments in the classroom is one way to familiarize IEP/ELLs with the process. Another is to develop and then use specific procedures for deciding what accommodations individual students need to participate in assessments. These suggestions and others, of course, may need to be adapted for IEP/ELLs.

INSTRUCTION FOR IEP/ELLs

Back to the bottom line! Students must be taught in order to perform well on tests. This is particularly true for students with disabilities who are limited in their English proficiency. Although our knowledge base on how best to teach IEP/ELLs is limited, we do know some things, and what we know is being increased by research. Applying even this little bit of knowledge will help students improve their achievement and test performances.

According to a comprehensive literature review conducted by Minnesota Assessment Project researchers within the National Center on Educational

Box 6.4

Considerations for Assessing LEP Students

- Teachers should regularly and frequently administer assessments, including assessments of English language proficiency for the purpose of monitoring the progress of English-language learners and for adapting instruction to improve performance.
- States and districts should develop clear guidelines for accommodations that permit English-language learners to participate in assessments administered for accountability purposes. Especially important are clear decision rules for determining the level of English-language proficiency at which English-language learners should be expected to participate exclusively in English-language assessments.
- Students should be assessed in the language that permits the most valid inferences about the quality of their academic performance. When numbers are sufficiently large, states and districts should develop subject-matter assessments in languages other than English.
- English-language learners should be exempted from assessments only when there is evidence that the assessment, even with accommodations, cannot measure the knowledge or skill of particular students or groups of students.
- States and districts should describe the methods they use to screen English-language learners for accommodations, exemptions, and alternate assessments, and they should report the frequency of these practices.
- Federal research units, foundations, and other funding agencies should promote research that advances knowledge about the validity and reliability of different accommodations, exemptions, and alternate assessment practices for English-language learners.

SOURCE: Reprinted with permission from Elmore, R. F., & Rothman, R. (Eds.) (1999). *Testing, teaching, and learning: A guide for states and school districts* (National Research Council report), p. 63. Washington, DC: National Academy Press.

Outcomes (NCEO) at the University of Minnesota, a variety of factors affects the test scores of IEP/ELLs. Among the factors identified by the literature were the following:

- *The degree of acculturation in the student*: the extent to which the student has acquired the customs and values of a culture.
- *The level of first and second language proficiency*: the level of social and academic language skills in both the first and second language.
- *The extent of cognitive development and literacy in the native language*: the extent to which the student has been exposed to schooling and other factors related to cognitive development.
- *Attitudinal factors*: beliefs about a variety of topics related to assessment, including attitudes about demonstrating knowledge, verbal communication, use of time, and so on.
- *Test bias*: in addition to language or cultural biases, there may be a bias in communicative style, cognitive style, or test interpretation.

Some of these factors are alterable and are affected by instruction, but others are not. It is important to identify those factors that are alterable in one's own situation and then to systematically identify ways to address the factors. These factors, of course, will also affect how students react to and profit from instruction.

When an ELL student has a diagnosed disability, he or she must be involved in at least three programs: general education, special education, and the ESL/bilingual program. It is critical that the three programs work with each other to form a seamless system for the student, one that does not have duplicated supports or gaps in support.

It is generally believed that effective instruction is good practice for all students (see Chapter 7 for more information on instruction).

Researchers Gersten and Fletcher, who have used different methodologies to identify effective instructional approaches for IEP/ELLs, show consensus on the following 10 approaches to instruction for these learners:

- Visuals to reinforce new concepts and vocabulary
- Rich and relevant vocabulary to keep students engaged and challenged
- Cooperative learning and peer tutoring strategies
- Strategic use of native language for introducing complex concepts
- Balance of linguistic and cognitive demands
- Clear and consistent language use when introducing new concepts
- Opportunities for learners to use both academic and conversational English
- Feedback that is adapted to the learner's level of language development
- Strong home–school connections
- Ongoing assessment of the effectiveness of instructional activities in producing student learning

A critical new consideration in providing instruction to IEP/ELLs is ensuring that it is based on content standards. In the past, this has been a challenge because many special educators and teachers of ELLs were not familiar with the content standards. This should no longer be true, but it never hurts to check. And, of course, it will be important to promote the participation of IEP/ELLs in general education content classes to the extent possible—and this may be more than you are now thinking is possible.

A recent study showed that the teachers of IEP/ELLs perceived certain strategies to be most effective for these students, and that they varied by content area. The strategies in Box 6.5 are based on results from one state and need to be replicated in other states, but they provide some guidance from teachers who started with their state standards and considered the needs of IEP/ELLs in instruction.

An important part of preparing IEP/ELLs to perform their best on state and district assessments is giving them the same advantages that other students have. As noted previously, general education students generally have picked up test preparation and test-taking strategies on their own. This is generally not the case for students with disabilities and is doubly not so for students who are ELLs.

Box 6.5	

Strategies Identified as Important for IEP/ELLs

Content Area	Strategy
Reading	Teaching pre-, during-, and post-reading strategies
	Fluency building (high frequency words)
	Direct teaching vocabulary through listening, seeing, reading, and writing in short time segments
	Relating reading to student experiences
	Chunking and questioning aloud (reading mastery)
Mathematics	Tactile, concrete experiences of mathematics
	Daily re-looping of previously learned material
	Problem solving instruction and task analysis strategies
	Teacher "think-alouds"
	Student "think-alouds"
Science	Hands-on, active participation
	Using visuals
	Using pictures to demonstrate steps
	Using pre-reading strategies in content areas
	Modeling/teacher demonstration

SOURCE: Reprinted with permission from Table 3, Importance of Strategies. In M. Thurlow, D. Albus, V. Shyyan, K. Liu, & M. Barrera (2004). *Educator perceptions of instructional strategies for standards-based education of English language learners with disabilities* (ELLs with Disabilities Report 7). Minneapolis: University of Minnesota, National Center on Educational Outcomes.

Thus, it is even more critical to ensure that IEP/ELL students know what to expect in the state or district test, and that they know how to prepare and take tests to their greatest advantage. Also, as noted before, this energy should not occur in place of regular instruction, but rather should be integrated into it. Still, checks should be done to make sure that the students are learning testing procedures as well as content.

SUMMARY

The IEP/ELL population, students with disabilities who are learning English, is perhaps one of the most challenging groups for our schools today. This is no excuse, however, for failing to give them the best education possible. Now is the time to quickly learn how to do this, because the numbers of these students are increasing and will continue to do so.

From what we now know, good instruction for any student is also good for IEP/ELLs. However, additional considerations must be given to these students because they have additional challenges. These challenges are related to language, the major way that we communicate information that we want students to learn. Thus, as educators, we need to rely on principles that ease the burden of language while still educating the child.

TEST YOUR KNOWLEDGE

Once again, review what you have learned in this chapter. Feel free to review the chapter and reread parts to fill in the blanks.

1. A common mistake is to equate students from non-English-language backgrounds with students who have limited English _____.

2. About 9.2% of all students who are ELLs are IEP/ELLs, but this is suspected to be an _____ estimate of the true population of these students.

3. The population of ELLs has grown dramatically in the United States during the past 10 years, much more rapidly than the _____ student population.

4. Overall, the special education category of _____ _____ is the most frequent in the IEP/ELL population across the United States.

5. Overall, _____ is the most prevalent first language of IEP/ELLs in the United States.

6. BICS refers to basic interpersonal _____ skills.

7. CALP refers to _____ academic language proficiency.

8. _____ often are needed by IEP/ELLs to address their needs related to both disabilities and ELL.

9. The need for data on the IEP/ELL subgroup becomes evident when trying to make good _____ decisions for these students.

10. It is critical that sufficient energy be devoted to making sure that IEP/ELLs know how to _____ for tests and how to take tests to their greatest advantage.

ANSWERS

1. proficiency (p. 100)

2. under (p. 101)

3. total (p. 102)

4. learning disabilities (p. 102)

5. Spanish (p. 103)

6. communication (p. 103)

7. cognitive (pp. 103)

8. Accommodations (p. 105)

9. instructional (p. 107)

10. prepare (p. 110)

REFLECTIONS ON CHANGE

See Appendix A for the Reflections on Change activity for this chapter (p. 191).

RECOMMENDED RESOURCES

Albus, D., & Thurlow, M.L. (2004). *Beyond subgroup reporting: English language learners with disabilities in 2002–2003 online state assessment reports* (ELLs with Disabilities Report 10). Minneapolis: University of Minnesota, National Center on Educational Outcomes.

August, D., & Hakuta, K. (Eds.) (1998). *Educating language-minority children.* National Research Council. Washington, DC: National Academy Press.

August, D., & Hakuta, K. (Eds.). (1997). *Improving schooling for language-minority children: A research agenda.* Washington, DC: National Academy Press.

Elmore, R. F., & Rothman, R. (Eds.). (1999). *Testing, teaching, and learning: A guide for states and school districts* (National Research Council report). Washington, DC: National Academy Press.

Fletcher, T., Bos, C., & Johnson, L. (1999). Accommodating English language learners with language and learning disabilities in bilingual education classrooms. *Learning Disabilities Research and Practice, 14,* 80–91.

Gersten, R., & Baker, S. (2000). What we know about effective instructional practices for English-language learners. *Exceptional Children, 66*(4), 454–470.

Gersten, R., Baker, S., & Marks, S. (1998). *Teaching English-language learners with learning difficulties: Guiding principles and examples from research-based practice.* Reston, VA: Council for Exceptional Children.

Liu, K., Thurlow, M., Erickson, R., & Spicuzza, R. (1997). *A review of the literature on students with limited English proficiency and assessment* (Minnesota Report 11). Minneapolis: University of Minnesota, National Center on Educational Outcomes.

National Clearinghouse on English Language Acquisition. (2003). *In the classroom: A toolkit for effective instruction of English language learners.* Available at www .ncela.gwu.edu/practice/itc/index.htm

National Research Council of the National Academies (2004) *Keeping score for all: The effects of inclusion accommodation policies on large-scale educational assessment.* Committee on Participation of English language learners and students with disabilities in NAEP and other large scale assessment. The National Academies Press: Washington, DC.

Ortiz, A. (1984). Choosing the language of instruction for exceptional bilingual children. *Teaching Exceptional Children, 16*(3), 202–206.

Rivera, C., Collum, E., Shafer, L., & Sia, J. K. (2004). *Analysis of state assessment policies regarding the accommodation of English language learners, SY 2000–2001.* Arlington, VA: George Washington University, Center for Equity and Excellence in Education.

Thurlow, M., Albus, D., Shyyan, V., Liu, K., & Barrera, M. (2004). *Educator perceptions of instructional strategies for standards-based education of English language learners with disabilities* (ELLs with Disabilities Report 7). Minneapolis: University of Minnesota, National Center on Educational Outcomes.

Thurlow, M., Minnema, J., & Treat, J. (2004). *A review of 50 states' online large-scale assessment policies: Are English language learners with disabilities considered?* (ELLs with Disabilities Report 5). Minneapolis: University of Minnesota, National Center on Educational Outcomes.

Zehler, A., Fleischman, H., Hopstock, P., Pendzick, M., & Stephenson, T., (2003). *Descriptive study of services to LEP students and LEP students with disabilities.* Arlington, VA: Development Associates.

INTERNET RESOURCES

Center for Research on Education, Diversity, & Excellence (CREDE): www.crede.ucsc.edu

Education Alliance (LAB): www.lab.brown.edu

National Association of Bilingual Education (NABE): www.nabe.org

National Center on Educational Outcomes (NCEO): www.nceo.info

National Clearinghouse for English Language Acquisition & Language Instruction Education Programs (NCELA): www.ncela.gwu.edu

Teachers of English to Students of Other Languages (TESOL): www.tesol.edu

4-6 Self-Check: Where Do I Stand?

Evaluate and reflect on the following statements as a personal survey of where you stand in relation to the information presented thus far. Base your responses to each survey on the topics that are presented in this book and what you think that you already know and are doing.

Self-Check for Chapter 4

- Like any other assessment, I understand the importance of using the results to improve instruction and programs for students. I am prepared to do that for my students.
- I understand the need and purpose for providing accommodations. I am familiar with those permitted on my district's and my state's assessments. I teach and reinforce those identified for students throughout my instruction with them.
- I understand that in the past there has been the tendency to overaccommodate students. When I am in question about those students who truly need a specific accommodation, I collect and chart performance data on the student. That is, I let the student use the accommodation, and I keep track of how the student uses the accommodations and performs.
- I am familiar with possible alternative routes to the diploma in my district or state. I know this is especially important for students who may fail a district or state test or be denied graduation or promotion as a result of the denial of a needed accommodation.

Self-Check for Chapter 5

- I have a plan for helping the students with disabilities in my class prepare for the district assessment. It involves both preparing for the test and providing information and practice on test-taking strategies.
- I know ways to encourage students to do well on tests, and I know how to avoid expectations that are damaging to student's self-concepts and to their test performances.

- I know how to promote strong but pleasant advocacy skills in my students with disabilities and am encouraging them to assert themselves in appropriate ways so that they will receive needed accommodations as they become more independent.

Self-Check for Chapter 6

- I know the policies that my district and state have in place for making decisions about IEP/ELLs, and I know how to implement those policies so that they result in the best decisions for students.
- I understand the importance of including all students in state and district assessments and know how to incorporate in my instruction ways to increase the test-taking skills of my IEP/ELLs.
- I recognize the need to look at the performance of the IEP/ELL subgroup, and I know that this helps in making better decisions about programs and instruction. I understand the importance of attending to standards-based instructional strategies that are effective for teaching these students both language and content.

Improving Performance on General Assessments Through Instruction

7

Perhaps there are teachers who think they have done a good day's teaching irrespective of what pupils have learned.

—*John Dewey, 1933*

The basic problem in achieving educational excellence is a misalignment among what teachers teach, what they think they teach, and what they assess as having been taught.

—*Susan Mulkey*

Hot-Button Issues

- All students can learn. Rhetoric or reality?
- What really works for teaching diverse learners in our classrooms?
- That special education student is on my class roster, and I don't feel I should be responsible for her. She will never reach proficiency on the state assessment.

Does instruction really matter, or do we just send all students through the curriculum and hope for the best? In this chapter, we will take a close look at where instruction fits in the national push for standards-based reform, accountability, and assessment. We will also look at what instruction should look like to improve student performance and, more important, to ensure that students learn.

In late 1980, the business community and postsecondary institutions of learning hoisted a flag. They announced that they were tired of admitting high school graduates who were unable to compete in the global workforce or to go to college without first receiving remedial coursework. In fact, high school graduates could not always read or complete simple math. The Business Roundtable was a group that made public its grave concern over the quality of the education of students in America's schools. Business corporations started conducting academic boot camps in an effort to raise the basic skills of new hires. Many consider the actions of the business community, in general, a major push behind public discussion and national concern over academic accountability.

At a specially convened meeting in 1989, the nation's governors and the U.S. President together agreed on six education goals. Reworked into eight education goals by Congress, these goals became a major piece of legislation in 1994, known as Goals 2000: Educate America Act. During the development of the law, national groups began to gather to establish standards in major areas such as mathematics, social studies, and science. Many of these national standards served as guideposts for beginning the task of establishing content standards for states and districts.

Today, No Child Left Behind (NCLB) has taken center stage in its attempt to continue to push the national education system to higher levels of accountability and results.

WHERE THE RUBBER MEETS THE ROAD

The role of teachers is not just to teach but also to create an environment where students can learn. Those of us who have taught students surely want credit for our successful students but not the blame for unsuccessful ones. After all, teaching is hard work, and on top of that, many students come to school from broken homes and low socioeconomic backgrounds. Yet other students who come to school may be chemically dependent or are in other psychological states that are not conducive to learning. Still others have not mastered fundamental skills or have poor or nonexistent work habits. The reasons (and excuses) for unsuccessful learners, in other words, are not hard to find.

However, we know more about teaching, and about how to teach special needs and at-risk students, than ever before. Yet many teachers are not using or even aware of this knowledge. Even more tragic, this knowledge and years of extensive research about what works for kids are not always present or apparent in classrooms. How many of you know teachers who "baby-sit" their students or give them little work or only easy work to do? This can happen for lots of reasons. One of the most prevalent reasons is the level of expectation (or the lack thereof). We are talking about those folks who really believe that students with special needs can't learn toward the standards that other kids are learning. And we must point out that this belief is prevalent in both general and special educator camps.

Consider this scenario: A special education teacher was at the school building's copy machine, making copies of pages from the Grade 9 algebra book (of course, this was because she had no books for her students!). A general education teacher looked over her shoulder and said *"Your* kids can do that?" We bet this sounds remotely familiar to some of you and needs little elaboration.

Over the past 30 years, since the inception of landmark special education laws, educators have created a dual system of teaching: one for general students and another for special education students. Although many thought a separation seemed appropriate, given the diversity and differences between general and special education students, professionals, parents, and students have come to know only too well the unanticipated outcomes of such a system. Over the years society has worked toward improvement in educating students with special needs. However, take a minute and think about the standards, curricula, and materials used in special education classrooms. Unfortunately, too many educators, especially special educators, still respond to this by saying "Standards? What curriculum? What materials?"

With today's push for accountability and assessment, one would think the standards, curriculum, and materials issues would be a situation of the past. More than ever before, the use of effective instruction connected to standards, curricular frameworks, and aligned assessments is vital to maximizing the performance of all students, including students with special needs.

THE REALITIES

Some would argue that it is quite ludicrous that we expect all ninth graders, for example, to be ready to complete a required course in algebra—especially when many arrive at the door of the high school not yet proficient in basic mathematic calculations. Alternately, how can we expect all third graders to be proficient readers by year's end? Of course, we know that these concerns are not due to students who have disabilities; rather they come to school with varied learning and teaching histories. Certainly other variables exist, such as attendance, discipline, mobility, and home environments. However, none preclude us from developing and implementing intervention programs to address these students who may be more at risk for failure, including those from low socioeconomic backgrounds.

The Long Beach Unified School District (LBUSD), the third largest urban district in southern California, has seriously taken on the charge of creating multiple pathways and interventions for all students. In 2004, LBUSD won the Broad Award and was deemed America's Best Urban School District. Although no small task, this award is a result of many years of dedication to educating urban schoolchildren who come from various and sundry backgrounds. According to the U.S. 2000 Census, Long Beach is considered the most diverse city in the country.

The Long Beach Unified School District has aggressively gone after reforms and initiatives to improve the performance of its K–12 population. Some of the instructional reforms include mandatory district benchmark assessments in Grades 1, 3, and 5. These benchmark assessments include math facts and reading. Those readers who do not pass these benchmarks are required to attend summer school that is focused on remediating and teaching students the skills they need to pass those benchmarks. If they are unable to pass the assessments, they are retained in a literacy classroom during the next year. These students simply do not repeat the same grade; rather they are enrolled into an 18:1 (or lower) student-teacher ratio classroom, staffed by highly skilled teachers who provide teaching and learning interventions that are targeted to student needs. Other reading interventions for K–5 include a districtwide, empirically based reading program, afterschool, Saturday school programs, and eight-week reading clinics. All of these interventions have been worth their weight in gold. As a result of the district's K–5 reading initiative and retention policy, the percentage of students entering middle school reading more than a year and a half below grade level dropped from 94% in 1999 to 48% in 2003. In 1999, 6.7% of all 5th graders were at grade level and in 2002—53.5% of all 5th graders were at grade level. (For more details, see www.LBUSD.k12.ca.us.)

High schools have been under reform for the past few years and have come out on top. All students in the high schools are enrolled in one of three tracks for literacy: intensive, strategic, or core. Every incoming ninth grader is assessed using multiple measures to determine placement. Based on those results they are scheduled into reading and English classes that target intervention in these areas. Students in the intensive and strategic tracks are given double doses of reading or math or both. The core students are those who are not in need of intervention. All students, including students with disabilities, are included in this high school initiative. And, at the printing of this book, all six comprehensive high schools, with enrollments anywhere from 3,900 to 4,700 students, made schoolwide 2004 adequate yearly progress (AYP)!

Another area of intervention is Algebra. This all too familiar core content area in high school has created huge challenges for many students. To address this issue, the district has provided an extended course in algebra from one year to two years (also known as "stretch algebra") to allow those students who need it more time to master the concepts.

Pushing all students to high standards no matter the socioeconomic background or situational context is a worthy goal and is absolutely possible with targeted resources and comprehensive intervention plans that encompass all students. We do also recognize the fact that this is not a one-size-fits-all world. However, schools, districts, and states have spent way too much time admiring the problem of why all students may not be expected to learn, instead of saying, We expect all students to learn, and here is how we are going to do it. We strongly believe that to hold schools accountable, district and state leaders must also be held accountable in the same public way. In this way we mean that accountability is reciprocal.

Imagine creating a standard that said "All people will wear size four shoes." Some of us would have great difficulty meeting that standard, and in many cases, it would cause great pain. Others could meet the standard by fitting half their foot in the shoe, while the rest hung out. The big question is what we would accomplish with a "size four shoe" standard? How valid would the performance standard be if some folks walked (or hobbled) around with half a foot hanging out of their shoe? What are we really trying to achieve here—uniformity, utility, or mediocrity? Herein lies the incredible importance of standard setting and targeted instructional interventions that reflect an overall purpose and includes all students, teachers, and administrators. It truly does take a village to raise achievement for all.

If we are genuinely concerned with educating all students to high standards, doesn't it make sense that we strive to work with individual student learning differences? Although our current educational system is one where time is the constant and learning is the variable, there are ways to address individual differences head on—effective instruction. Students don't all "get it" at the same time. For example, we could all participate in a 5K run and finish it. Some runners would be way ahead of others. Some would run the entire route, while others would run and walk the course. But in the end, we would all cross the finish line. The reality of this example in our schools is that resources (or lack thereof), teachers, time, and budget constraints all impact our run for the finish. And we know that is it more cost efficient for students to take one type of test, for example, multiple choice, than providing students with different individualized ways to show what they know. So all students, both general education and special education, can learn the standards, but they may better show what they know and can do if provided with more time to learn via effective instruction and thoughtful methods of assessment.

THE MILLION-DOLLAR QUESTION

The state assessments are too hard for special education students! Why would we make students with disabilities take them? Let's take a look at that question more closely. There are at least three basic reasons that folks think the state assessments are useless or too hard for students with disabilities: (1) students have not learned the content, (2) the format of the test is such that it impedes the students' ability to show what they know, and (3) students need accommodations not allowed on the test.

First, we must ask why students have not learned the content. Is it a result of lowered expectations? Perhaps lack of exposure or opportunity to learn the material? If the ultimate goal for all students is to graduate with a high school diploma as a result of completing the same course requirements as all other students, why aren't they learning the same content standards? A number of states still allow students with disabilities to graduate with a diploma if they attain their Individualized Education Program (IEP) goals and objectives. An unintended outcome of this policy is that educators are more likely to feel less pressure or responsibility for students with disabilities to learn the same standards because they will receive the same diploma regardless.

The second issue of test format is perhaps trickier. We can impact the quality of instruction and the use and provision of accommodations, but we can't alter the format of the state assessments. That decision is at the state and legislative levels. That is why the appropriate consideration of accommodations is so critical for students with disabilities and those on Section 504 (of the Rehabilitation Act of 1973) plans.

Finally, there are several landmark cases that have challenged the denial of accommodations on state assessments. (See Chapter 4 for specifics.) The trend now is to provide students their civil right of using needed accommodations on assessments and then figure out how to score and where to report these assessment results. However, in some states, if a student uses a nonstandard accommodation (also referred to as a modification), the assessment is automatically scored "far below proficient." It is a matter of time before that is challenged by the courts, just as the denial of the use of needed accommodations for assessments has been.

Although we don't have an easy one-size-fits-all answer to the million dollar question, we do know where to start to look—instruction. What do the instructional practices and methodologies look like? What is really going on in the classroom? Are empirically based practices of effective instruction taking place in all classrooms? Do the practices include thorough planning, managing, delivering, and evaluating of instruction? After all, we can only blame the assessments for so long, and then it's time to take a critical look at what is going on in the classroom.

PREPARING FOR INSTRUCTION: THE PLANNING PYRAMID

Teaching is complex. Teachers make thousands of decisions every day. Deciding what to teach and how to teach for each student makes teachers' jobs even more tricky. Consider the basic components of the instructional planning pyramid. There are lots of ways to think about standards-based instruction. Not all of them lead to structured, thorough planning. Introduced by Schumm, Vaughn, and Leavell (1994), the concept of a pyramid provides a visualization of the context, topic, and instructional practices that are needed by students (Box 7.1). It also enables you to consider the information or curriculum that all students should learn, what most students will learn, and what some students will learn.

One of the strengths of the pyramid is that it provides a way to think of standards-based instruction within the context of students' abilities. That is, some students will naturally need extensions or more in-depth coverage of topics. And there will be others who will work to learn the basic elements of a concept or strategy.

Whether a student learns at the base, middle, or top of the pyramid is not determined by a student's ability. Unlike some current practices where students with disabilities are sentenced to a particular curriculum or set of teaching methodologies, the instructional planning pyramid takes into consideration a student's prior knowledge. That is, student's skills and interests will vary by the topic introduced. For example, some of us are more excited than others to learn algebraic equations, biophysics, or mythology. In the same manner, students' interests will influence their excitement and ease with which they learn topics. Knowing this can help you plan your instruction differently. The context is also important. Consider learning mythology on the steps of one of the ruins in Greece. That could make it at least tolerable, don't you think? In the same manner, students need a context of where and how the learning will be important and useful. Context matters. Instructional practices should reflect the student, topic, and context of instruction. Therefore, we offer some orienting questions for use with the planning pyramid concept (Box 7.2).

> **Box 7.1**
>
> ### Components of the Instructional Planning Pyramid
>
>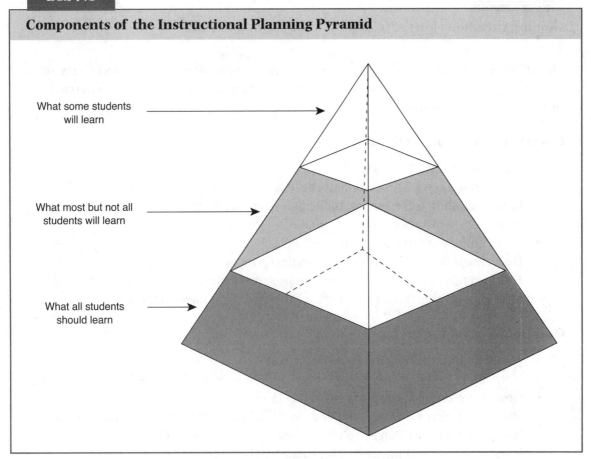
>
> What some students will learn
>
> What most but not all students will learn
>
> What all students should learn

The instructional planning pyramid is just one way to look at the breadth and depth of what you teach and its relevance for all students. It is important that you decide the bottom line for all students. What do you expect all students to master? Most? Some?

WHAT DO WE KNOW ABOUT EFFECTIVE INSTRUCTION?

In most cases, when a student does not progress through the curriculum at the expected rate, the child is placed under a microscope. That is, the student is usually referred for psychoeducational evaluation that almost always focuses on what skills the student lacks. Seldom does the evaluation examine classroom factors that may in fact be directly linked to the student's lack of progress. What is often missing is evaluation of the instructional environment. Variables that are explored in such an analysis are those known to be directly related to academic success, such as academic engaged time, opportunities to respond, teacher presentation style, teacher-student monitoring procedures, academic learning time, and teacher expectations, to name of few. Without a comprehensive evaluation of the student within the context of the instructional environment, it is often impossible to validly indicate the real cause of poor student progress.

Box 7.2

Guiding Questions for the Instructional Planning Pyramid

The following questions can be used in a self-questioning process to guide decision making when considering topics of instruction, readiness to teach the material, and student readiness to receive the instruction.

Questions Pertaining to the Topic

- Is the material new or review?
- What prior knowledge do students have of this topic?
- How interesting is the topic to individual students? To me?
- How many new concepts are introduced?
- How complex are the new concepts?
- How clearly are concepts presented in the textbook?
- How can this material be connected to previous instruction? Can it?
- How important is this topic or parts of the topic for students to learn?

Questions Pertaining to the Teacher

- Have I taught this material before?
- How can I evaluate whether students are learning what I am teaching?
- How interesting is the topic to students? To me?
- How can students' cultural and linguistic backgrounds be connected to the topic?
- How much time do I have to plan for the unit and individual lessons?
- What resources do I have available to me for this unit?

Questions Pertaining to Students

- Will students' communication skills make comprehension of a particular topic or concept difficult?
- Will students with reading difficulties be able to work independently while learning about the concept from the text?
- Will a student with behavior or attention problems be able to concentrate on this material?
- Which students will likely have high interest in or prior knowledge of this concept or be anxious to explore this topic in greater breadth and depth?
- What experiences have the students had that will relate to this concept?
- Is there some way to relate this concept to the cultural and linguistic backgrounds of the students?

Teachers today are expected to raise the test scores of an increasingly diverse group of students, teach huge amounts of content, and manage a wide range of behaviors, almost certainly with limited resources.

The good news is that research on effective instruction has been going on for years. Most of this research focuses on general education settings. However,

Box 7.3

Some Research-Based Findings on Characteristics of Effective Practices

A cross-case analysis in Massachusetts Urban public schools (Donahue Institute, 2004) identified practices essential to state test success of students with special needs. The following is a generalized (non-Massachusetts) version of the practices identified:

- Pervasive emphasis on curriculum alignment to state standards
- Effective system to support curriculum alignment
- Emphasis on inclusion and access to curriculum
- Culture and practices that support high standards and student achievement
- Well disciplined academic and social environment
- Use of student assessment data to inform decision making
- Unified practice supported by targeted professional development
- Access to resources to support key initiatives
- Effective staff recruitment, retention, and deployment
- Flexible leaders and staff who work effectively in a dynamic environment
- Effective leadership that is essential to success

recent research has identified similiar effective practices for special needs students (Box 7.3).

Improving Student Performance: A Model of Effective Instruction

To maximize student learning and achievement, we believe you must first delve into instructional practices. In this section, we provide a research-based model of effective instruction that emphasizes principles, strategies, and tactics. A practical model presented by Algozzine, Ysseldyke, and Elliott (1997) includes four components on how to plan, manage, deliver, and evaluate instruction in the classroom. Note that for each component there is a set of empirically demonstrated principles and strategies of effective instruction (Box 7.4).

In this section, we outline each of the four components and corresponding principles. For each principle we have a "Think About It" box. This box is just one of the many ways this model can be used to deliver valuable techniques and tactics to the classroom for the improvement of student learning. For more information about strategies and tactics for effective instruction, see the Recommended Resources section at the end of the chapter.

PLANNING INSTRUCTION

Principles

- Decide what to teach.
- Decide how to teach.
- Communicate realistic expectations.

Box 7.4

Components of Effective Instruction	
Planning instruction	The degree to which teaching goals and teacher expectations for student performance and success are stated clearly and are understood by the student
Managing instruction	The degree to which classroom management is effective and efficient
	The degree to which there is a sense of positiveness in the school environment
Delivering instruction	The degree to which there is an appropriate instructional match
	The degree to which lessons are presented clearly and follow specific instructional procedures
	The degree to which instructional support is provided for the individual student
	The degree to which sufficient time is allocated to academics and instructional time is used efficiently
	The degree to which the student's opportunity to respond is high
Evaluating instruction	The degree to which the teacher actively monitors student progress and understanding
	The degree to which student performance is evaluated appropriately and frequently

SOURCE: Reprinted with permission from Sopris West (Algozzine, Ysseldyke, & Elliott, 1997).

Seems reasonable and simple, doesn't it? Planning for instruction is the backbone of effective instruction; the rest follows. You need to know what to teach in order to plan. A great place to start is the standards and curricular frameworks established by your district and/or state. Guess what? Instructional results are better when instruction is planned. As previously mentioned, one of the characteristics of norm-referenced tests (NRTs) is the lack of overlap in what is taught and what is tested (the overlap has been estimated to be approximately 20%). Although many states now use standards-based assessments, most still also use NRTs. One sure way to plan for the ultimate fruits of instructional labor, student achievement, is to examine the scope and sequence of the test and decide what must be instructed and with what kinds of emphasis (see Chapter 2 for a discussion of backmapping). Three principles for effective planning exist: deciding what to teach, deciding how to teach, and communicating realistic expectations (cf. Algozzine et al., 1997).

Deciding What to Teach

In deciding what to teach, teachers must have a firm grasp on the scope and sequence of the curriculum and skills needed to demonstrate proficiency or mastery of the content material. Effective educators accomplish this by working to match the students' level of skill development with the level of instruction. Be sure to look at beginning, middle, and end of the tasks for the hierarchy of skills, if any, needed to complete them. In addition, it is also important to take into consideration the need for instructional accommodation. Organization of the instructional environment is also important and includes the physical layout of the classroom, peer interactions, instructional grouping arrangements, and the like. The goal of deciding what to teach is accurately determining the appropriate content to present, matching the students' instructional levels, and using high expectations to guide learning and teaching. Think about it (Box 7.5).

Box 7.5

Deciding What to Teach: Think About It

- Prioritizing standards
- Starting with skills that are needed to learn other skills
- Identifying types of knowledge needed and teaching all of them

The breadth and depth of a curriculum can be overwhelming when you think about the actual number of days of instruction within which learning must occur. Given this reality, it is critical to prioritize those standards and skills students need to acquire. Give top priority to those skills that are hierarchical in nature, that is, those that are needed and essential to the performance of more complex skills.

Three basic types of knowledge exist: factual, conceptual, and strategic. **Factual knowledge** involves things like rote learning simple facts (H_2O is water; $20 \times 2 = 40$), verbal chains (saying the alphabet), and discrimination. Factual knowledge can be demonstrated without a student understanding how to figure out how the answer was derived ($20 \times 2 = 40$, not two sets of 20).

Conceptual knowledge involves students understanding the meaning and critical attributes. For example, what are the critical attributes of a square? What are the critical attributes of a mathematical word problem? We often lose students when we move from factual to conceptual. Try it with students; have a student explain how he got the answer to $20 \times 2 = 40$. Can he or she explain it is two sets of 20 items or 20 sets of two? Or what is absolutely necessary to solve the word problem? Or even what are the noncritical attributes or distracters in the word problem? You will be surprised what you will find out.

Strategic knowledge involves using a procedure, plan, or steps in the process to solve problems, perform tasks, or derive answers. Strategic knowledge can range from how to solve a mathematics equation to how to find Malawi, Africa, on a map. How do we do that? By using a strategy, of course! So although students may be able to come up with the correct answer to simple questions, they may not have the ability to explain how they arrived at the answer.

Identifying the types of knowledge required for specific assignments and tasks doesn't mean that a task has only one type of knowledge. On the contrary, many things we ask students to identify or produce have all three types of knowledge. For example, multiplying three-digit by two-digit numbers requires the use of facts, the concept of multiplication, and the strategy of actually solving the problem.

(Continued)

(Continued)

Think about how this fits into preparing students for assessments. We usually know ahead of time by looking at a test matrix (for district/state tests) or, because we developed the test, what types of questions will be asked and how many. The importance here is that you understand the types of knowledge you are teaching and are able to identify them when students have difficulties.

Deciding How to Teach

Teaching can be an experimental process. Teaching students involves gathering data or information on the kinds of things that do and do not work. Deciding how to teach involves making educated guesses about what might work with some students. Although many methods are touted as the best way to teach, not everything works for every student. What we do know is that basic elements exist for preparing how to teach. They include setting instructional goals, selecting methods and materials, determining the pace of instruction, and deciding how student participation and performance will be monitored. The goal of deciding how to teach is finding the best way to present desired and/or required instructional content teaching. Think about it (Box 7.6).

Box 7.6

How to Teach: Think About It

- Identify skills that are hierarchical in nature or are foundation skills.
- Identify students' levels of proficiency.
- Monitor and adjust instruction to move students to next level of proficiency.

To plan effectively, it is good practice to identify the proficiency level at which the student is working. Three basic levels exist: accuracy, mastery, and automaticity. If a student is learning new material or lacks knowledge on a task, she is at the initial phase of learning called **acquisition**. Student progress is often slow, and correctness will be less than 80%. Another student may be able to perform work correctly but at a slow rate. This student needs fluency instruction that facilitates mastery—accurate and fast. Finally, all instruction is aimed to have students use a skill independently and automatically when needed. This is called **generalization**. We know this does not happen automatically for many students. Therefore, they need to be taught how to transfer the use of skills to other related tasks or different settings.

Why is this important? Think about assessment. Often certain sections of a test are timed. Are students being taught fluency and speed skills in order to pace themselves through these sections? Do they have a sense of time? What about during instruction? Do you have a sense of where every student is in terms of acquisition of skills? Are they able to generalize and integrate information and skill to other topics? This is obviously a critical skill in essay writing and performance events. Does your instruction reflect and consider levels of proficiency?

Communicating Realistic Expectations

Expectations for success must be clearly communicated. Set them high, but be sure they are attainable. Think about a time you enrolled in a graduate class. What was the first thing you were interested in? If you are like most people, you said the course syllabus. Most graduate students want to know how to get an A, whether there will be a final or midterm, and so on. Things are no different for students in schools today. It is essential that they know what is expected of them every step of the way. Think about it: do you start every lesson by telling your students what they will learn, why they will learn it, and how mastery will be shown? The goal of communicating realistic expectations is providing clear communication of high realistic expectations, so that everybody is on the same page and no one's needs are overlooked or missed while teaching. Think about it (Box 7.7).

Box 7.7

Communicate Realistic Expectations: Think About It

- Tell students what they will learn.
- Tell students why it is important to learn.
- Tell students how good is good enough.

Effective educators tell their students what they are expected to know and be able to do and to what level of proficiency. These educators do this at the start of every lesson. When preparing students for any assessment or test, it is imperative they know what to expect, what will be covered, and how (multiple choice, performance event, etc.). Not only does it keep students accountable but teachers as well. One of the keys to improving student performance is communicating to students what they must know and then providing them the road map to get there. It is like a trip. We know where we are going and the way to go, but how do we know when we arrived?

MANAGING INSTRUCTION

Principles

- Prepare for instruction.
- Use time productively.
- Establish positive classroom environment.

In the Algozzine et al. (1997) model, managing instruction is not about managing student behavior per se. Managing instruction refers to how efficient and effective classrooms routines are. That is, there is a presence of cooperation, structure, and order. Effective instruction requires managing a complex mix of instructional tasks and student behaviors. This means making decisions that control and support an orderly flow of instruction. After all, it is hard to teach students anything if they aren't in their seats or attending to task. And how much learning can really occur in classrooms that are unstructured and chaotic? Effective managing is accomplished through three principles: Prepare for instruction, use time productively, and establish a positive classroom teaching environment.

Preparing for Instruction

Effective teachers establish classroom rules and expectations, communicate them early in the year, and throughout the year. They teach students the consequences of following and not following classroom rules and procedures. Rule infractions and other classroom disruptions are handled as quickly as possible after they occur. One of the ultimate goals of managing instruction is to have students manage their own behavior. A goal of preparing for instruction is to try to anticipate, avoid, and address problems that might disrupt the orderly flow of instruction teaching. Think about it (Box 7.8).

Box 7.8

Prepare for Instruction: Think About It

- Prepare students for instruction.
- Provide opportunities for students to show what they know and can do.
- Make teaching fun.

A fun instructional tactic to use with the whole class is called the Good Behavior Game, but it really isn't a game. Simply divide the class into two teams; be sure they are balanced for skill and ability. Identify one to three behaviors or skills that need improvement or will be taught. Decide on the criteria you will use to evaluate whether the behavior or skills have been demonstrated. Discuss both the target skills and criteria with students so they understand what is expected and what they need to demonstrate to get points for their team. Then let the game begin! For example, the class may need to work on responding to questions, working cooperatively, and work completion. During instruction, multiple opportunities are provided for students to demonstrate the behaviors, and tallies are kept for both sides. Teams can see who has more tallies and work to compete for the most points. What do they win? That is up to you. For most students, the satisfaction of being on the winning team is enough. Some teachers keep track of points and teams work for some incentive to be delivered after a week or so. Another example of this technique can be to list skills such as reading for comprehension, correctly solving algebraic equations, or using correct strategies or steps to solve problems. Anything goes. You can work on behavior or skills in a format in which progress in posted publicly and teamwork is developed.

In preparing students for assessments, you can adapt the Good Behavior Game by using facts, concepts, or strategies that they will be required to know to perform well. It can be used during initial instruction or for review. This "game" is merely a technique to help students focus on behaviors and skills that need attention. Try it. Be creative.

Using Time Productively

Effective educators make decisions that maximize the amount of time students spend actively engaged in learning. They minimize the time spent on activities not related to learning. There is evidence to suggest that students often spend more time in transition than engaged in learning. It is imperative that teachers establish routines and procedures, including transition time, and allocate time to activities that maintain an academic focus. The goal of using time productively is maximizing the time teachers spend teaching and students spend learning. Think about it (Box 7.9).

Box 7.9

Use Time Productively: Think About It

- Allocate time for instruction.
- Check your instructional time for actual engaged student learning.
- Provide instruction that actively engages students in learning.

How is instruction time in your classes allocated? Allocated learning time is defined as the amount of time set aside for **engaged** student learning. Daily classroom schedules should be allocated by three basic rules of thumb: (1) The instructional day or class period should allocate at least 70% for student learning, (2) the amount of time students are to be engaged in learning should be about 85%, and (3) the rate of accuracy of students' engaged work should be around 80%. A quick formula to check your allocated learning time is the total amount of time in an instructional day or class period multiplied by 0.7. For example, 6.5-hour school day × 0.7 = 4.6 hours. That means that 4.6 hours of the day need to be devoted to active engaged student learning. Another example, (50-minute class period) × (0.7) = 35 minutes should be allocated to engaged student learning.

Check your daily instructional classes to see how much time students actually spend in engaged learning. It is not enough to say social studies is taught from 1 to 1:50 p.m. every day. We need to be able to identify how that 50 minutes of student learning are spent. What we have found in working with teachers in these areas is that more time is spent in transition than realized, or little time is allocated to guided practice with students. The connection to this and improving student performance on assessment should be clear. The more we engage students in what they should know and be able to do, the better they will perform.

Establishing a Positive Classroom Environment

It has been said that students learn three to four times more when they are motivated to learn. Most children and youth (and adults) perform better when teachers interact positively with them. Motivation is built through supportive and helpful learning environments. Students (and adults) like school more when their classrooms are pleasant, friendly places. And students will work better when they like their teachers! Effective educators are accepting and caring and strive for positive interaction that fosters active student responding. The goal of

Box 7.10

Establishing a Positive Classroom Environment: Think About It

- Keep a positive attitude—it's contagious.
- Teach students that one can learn from making mistakes.
- Use positive praise statements.

Did you know that the more students like and respect you, the harder they will work? Think about that as adults. Do we not tend to stick it out with people—colleagues and friends—when we respect them? We can't forget that this holds true for the students we teach. Teaching is tough, and sometimes we forget to let students know how much we care about them and the work they are doing. How often do you tell students how much you appreciate them? We know that some days are harder than others, but this is still a critical piece of the instructional process. Improving student performance is inextricably linked to how students feel about themselves and the support they feel, their self-concept, and their abilities to take risks.

Making personalized statements to students about their efforts and perseverance is important. Consider this statement: "Wow, José you did a great job!" What does this really say? Does this reflect the time and thought José put into the task? What about "Wow, José. Nice job sticking to the assignment. Look at the results of your labor!" We encourage you to think about how you recognize student efforts. To motivate a learner, students must see the connection between their efforts and the fruits of their labor, no matter how small.

establishing a positive classroom environment is creating a place where students like to be, feel supported, and enjoy learning. Think about it (Box 7.10).

DELIVERING INSTRUCTION

Principles

- Present information.
- Monitor presentations.
- Adjust presentations.

Teaching is the systematic presentation of content necessary for mastery of the subject matter. Good teaching doesn't just happen. It involves careful planning to decide what and how to teach as well as providing a smooth flow of classroom rules, routines, and procedures that are conducive for student learning. Delivering instruction involves presenting information while monitoring student understanding of what is being taught. This means that teachers are constantly planning how to present information while keeping track of student performance and adjusting instruction to accommodate for individual differences. Three principles exist for effectively delivering instruction: Present information, monitor presentations, and adjust teaching to accommodate the needs of students (cf. Algozzine et al., 1997).

Presenting Information

Empirically demonstrated ways exist for presenting instruction. Effective educators interact positively with their students to gain and maintain attention, review previously taught material, provide organized lessons, and introduce new material by connecting it to students' prior knowledge. Among other things, brisk pacing and checking students' understanding are all vital to presenting information to students. When teaching thinking skills, for example, effective teachers model ways to solve problems. When motivating students, effective teachers use extrinsic incentives with enthusiasm. Teachers always keep in mind that the ultimate goal of motivating students is to get them to become intrinsically motivated or reduce the tangible incentives to a minimum. When providing practice, effective teachers provide relevant but varied opportunities to practice and provide time needed by students to do so. Teachers use a variety of activities when providing both guided and independent practice. The goal in presenting information is to teach students new information or to extend or reinforce previous knowledge. Think about it (Box 7.11).

Box 7.11

Presenting Information: Think About It

- Be creative.
- Extend students' learning and abilities in creative, fun ways.
- Provide activities that integrate students' learning.

Teachers can incorporate many different techniques to get students motivated and excited about learning, and provide opportunities to practice what they have learned. Here is a favorite: Teach students how to create license plates for the topic of study they are learning. California is known for its "vanity license plates" that have snappy sayings about the people who are driving the car. You know the ones you try to figure out when you are stopped behind them; then they drive away before you can figure out what the license plate was trying to say. For instruction, try having the students create one on a specific topic. For example, students studying Civil War could create a license plate for a soldier (if he had a car!). Another example would be a license plate for a scientist who worked on the discovery of atom fusion. It sounds easier than it appears. You must have command of the subject as well as understand the facts, concepts, and strategies in order to apply it to this creative task.

Monitoring Presentations

When providing feedback to students, effective teachers provide immediate and frequent information that supports students' efforts to derive correct responses. Effective teachers model corrective procedures and methods for making improvements. When keeping students involved in lessons, teachers find ways to regularly monitor responses and use peer-mediated activities to provide ample and varied opportunities for learning. The goal in monitoring presentations is to ensure students are learning the content as it was intended. Think about it (Box 7.12).

Adjusting Presentations

The principle of adjusting presentations involves making decisions about how to change or modify instruction for students. Effective teachers use a variety of teaching strategies; they monitor and adjust the instructional pace to accommodate the individual needs of students, monitor student understanding, and stick with students until they have had the time to master what has been taught. Instructional information gathered throughout this process is in turn used to adjust instruction so that all students can meet with success. The goal of adjusting presentations is to make necessary instructional changes to guarantee that all students profit from instruction. Think about it (Box 7.13).

Box 7.12

Monitoring Presentation: Think About It

- Keep students actively involved.
- Find ways to assess student knowledge that aren't cumbersome.
- Provide lots of opportunities to show what they have learned.

Here is a technique that enables you to monitor student learning as well as provide students with a structured opportunity to expand their knowledge about a topic. We call it Chat-Check-Change. Have students stand in two concentric circles. Students on the inside circle face outward, while students on the outside circle face in. Pose a question or topic to the students, and say "go." Students on the inside circle must chat for 60 to 90 seconds about the question. When the time is up, say "stop" and tell the circles to move. The inside circle moves to the right, while the outside circle walks to the left. Tell students to stop and face their partners. Pose the same question or topic again. This time the students on the outside talk for 60 to 90 seconds. After this sharing, the teacher discusses the answer to the question or topic with the entire group. In this manner, both student circles have the opportunity to chat about the subject, relearning and extending the knowledge of facts, concepts, and strategies occur during this activity.

For the purpose of assessments, Chat-Check-Change enables the opportunity to review information for the test and it gives students the opportunity to learn information they may not have been aware of or understood. It is a great way to provide an active practice of learning.

Box 7.13

Adjusting Presentations: Think About It

- Teaching is orchestrating what and how we teach with how students learn.
- Consider the types of knowledge and the levels of proficiency when adjusting instruction.
- Tailor-made teaching strategies improve student achievement.

It is important to monitor how students are doing in instruction. It all gets tied together when we monitor students for the type of knowledge we are teaching, the level of proficiency they are at, and what instructional techniques make the most sense to improve student performance. It is about adjusting and aligning student learning and instruction. The following chart is a useful summary to help in pinpointing how to teach for student learning.

Types of Knowledge					
Accuracy		*Mastery*		*Accuracy*	
Entry Level	*Initial Advanced*	*Proficiency*	*Maintenance*	*Generalization*	*Adaption*
Absence of skill or low frequency (10% correct)	10%–25% correct / 26%–64% correct / 65%–90% correct	High rate of speed and accuracy above 90%	Fast and accurate (90%–100% correct)	Spontaneous transfer to new settings/ conditions	Higher-order thinking and problem solving
Instructional Tactics:	**Instructional Tactics:**	**Instructional Tactics:**	**Instructional Tactics:**	**Instructional Tactics:**	**Instructional Tactics:**
• Assessment	• Direct instruction • Demonstrating successful approximations • Modeling levels of cueing/ prompting • Specific directions • Feedback	• Drill practice modeling— fast and accurate • Specific reinforcement and praise	• Periodic checks and review • Direct instruction as needed	• Teach for generalization. • Direct instruction in a variety of settings and conditions. • Vary instructors.	• Teach creative problem solving. • Vary question types. • Use "What if?"
Skill Identification	**Skill Acquisition**	**Skill Fluency**	**Skill Retention**	**Skill Expansion**	**Skill Extension**

EVALUATING INSTRUCTION

Principles

- Monitor student understanding.
- Monitor engaged time.
- Keep records of student progress.
- Use data to make decisions.

The fourth component of effective instruction is evaluating the results of that instruction (see Chapter 3 for a complete discussion of data use). Effective instruction requires evaluating, which is the process of deciding whether the approaches, methods, and material used work with your students. Information gathered from effective evaluation is used to make decisions about whether to refer students to other student support services, change or modify interventions, or help determine whether a student can be exited from a program (such as exited from special education services or remedial reading programs). Evaluation completes the integral and valuable cycle in effective instructional processes and also feeds the instructional process. The evaluation of student progress should be ongoing and take place throughout instruction as well as at the end of a lesson or unit of study. Effective evaluating has four principles: Monitor student understanding, monitor engaged time, keep records of student progress, and use data to make teaching decisions (Algozzine et al., 1997).

Monitoring Student Understanding

The goal here is to keep track of and decide the extent to which students have benefited from instruction. This involves using a variety of ways to check with students to see whether they have really understood what has been taught. The goal here is to push students beyond the superficial level of learning to make sure they can show what they know. Think about it (Box 7.14).

Box 7.14

Monitor Student Understanding: Think About It

- Use a variety of techniques to check for student understanding.
- Keep track of what works.
- Be certain students understand.

HDYKT! That is, How Do You Know That? This simple technique forces students not only to give an answer but also to tell how they got it. Too often teachers hear the correct answer and move on without determining how students derived the answer. It isn't unusual to use HDYKT only to find out the answer is correct, but the strategy for deriving the answer is incorrect or lacking. Preparing students for short-answer or essay tests is not an easy task. This technique assists in expanding students' breadth and depth of information.

Monitoring Engaged Time

The concept of monitoring engaged time involves keeping track of the rate of student participation during instruction. The goal of monitoring engaged time is to determine the extent to which all students are actively and appropriately engaged in relevant instructional activities. Think about it (Box 7.15).

Box 7.15

Monitoring Engaged Time: Think About It

- Don't sit, but wander.
- Provide opportunities for students to be actively involved in learning.
- Teach—monitor—assess—teach.

All Write! Often teachers teach a lesson and don't stop to check for understanding. Although students may appear they are engaged, they may not be. This technique keeps students on their toes. During a lecture, stop and do an "All Write." Simply ask students to write a quick response to a posed question. Give students about a minute to jot down responses, including that they don't know. Walk around the room while students are writing. Then ask students to share responses. This technique is about identifying which students are on track as well as identifying information that needs clarification or more instruction. It provides students with a timed response—they have to quickly respond to the question.

Improving student performance is about making sure students are learning. We can't be sure of that unless we check for understanding and monitor our instruction. This becomes a challenge given the amount of information, standards, and curriculum that must be taught. However, the time it takes to check for engaged learning and understanding is worth its weight in test scores.

Keeping Records of Student Progress

Effective teachers keep track of student achievement and performance by using a variety of evaluative procedures. In addition, they routinely share this information with students. The goal of keeping records of student progress is to stay on top of student achievement as well as to keep the teachers informed about their teaching efforts. Think about it (Box 7.16).

Using Data to Make Decisions

Student data or progress should be used to make decisions about what is or is not working. The information gathered here can assist in making decisions about what additional assistance may be needed or, even better, no longer needed for students. The priority here is to use student data to make decisions that provide more or different support and/or instruction for students. Think about it (Box 7.17).

Keep Records of Student Progress: Think About It

- Vary evaluative procedures.
- Keep assessments easy, quick, and informative.
- Use assessments to drive instruction.

Use two-minute papers. At the end of class, have students each complete a two-minute paper and hand it in. They simply take two minutes to respond to the following statements.

1. Something I learned, relearned, or rediscovered as a result of this lesson is . . .

2. Something I am still confused about or need clarification on is . . .

Students have two minutes to complete both sentences. At the end of two minutes, they put their pens down or may finish a thought and then stop. Collect the papers, and you will have an understanding of how well you did in instructing students and how well they understood. It also provides you with a planning tool for your next day's lesson—where to reteach, review, or reinforce.

This technique simply keeps you informed about how students are learning. After all, that is what counts when improving student performance and making progress through the curriculum and standards.

Today, more than ever before, teachers are faced with the responsibility of educating increasingly diverse students. Teachers are expected to assist all students in meeting high standards in all content areas. Although empirically demonstrated principles of learning and teaching exist, difficulties can be experienced when implementing them. Teachers across the nation report that they don't have the time or resources to implement such principles. As is common with anything new, comprehension and implementation of this model of effective instruction may at first glance seem overwhelming. Remember the first time you tried to read or make sense of a student's IEP? It is the same phenomenon. It is overwhelming at first but becomes automatic after practice.

The Algozzine et al. (1997) model of effective instruction provides a systematic and structured approach for linking research-based principles of learning and teaching to classroom strategies and tactics. Grounded in the findings of educational research, the components and principles of this model provide a structure for organizing, understanding, and applying strategies and tactics used by effective teachers. The model is a flexible instructional improvement tool that can be used to make the connections between standards, curriculum, and assessments. The best way to improve instruction is to decide which principles of instruction are the most important in your situation and work on those first. Doing this necessarily involves selecting one of the components (planning,

Box 7.17

Use Data to Make Decisions: Think About It

- Don't guess, assess!
- Chart student progress.
- Use student performance to make instructional decisions about what next.

Too often we think students aren't getting it, so we change our technique or move on. And too often we continue to use a technique or method that is ineffective because that's the way we have always done it, or we think students will get it eventually. It's too much of a guessing game, don't you think? This scenario happens because we don't keep progress data on exactly how students are learning.

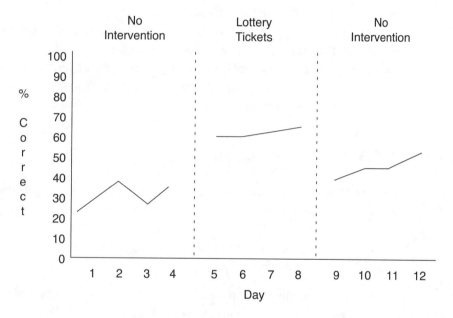

It should be clear how valuable this technique is to improving student performance. The *aimline* takes the guesswork out of how students are performing and the rate at which they are learning information. Aimlines may be more necessary with some students than others. Aimlines also can be used to set group or classroom goals as well. They provide both students and teachers with a visual tracking system for connecting performance to the end goal of instruction. Depending on the age of the students, they could record their progress on their own charts.

SOURCE: Elliott, Algozzine, and Ysseldyke (1998).

managing, delivering, or evaluating) and working on the principle within it first. By initially working on only one component and respective principles, strategies, and tactics, the task of improving instruction and ultimately student achievement is more systematic and manageable.

SUMMARY

In this chapter, we explored the key elements of maximizing student achievement by way of effective instruction. Nationally, the focus on assessment has created heightened tension and stress in the teaching force. Some argue that the breadth and depth of what gets taught in the classroom is directly related to what gets tested. If this in fact is true, why is it that so many students are still performing lower than expected and desired? Educators and other professionals can only blame the state or district assessments for so long; then they must direct their attention to what matters: instruction. To maximize the performance of all students, including students with disabilities, teachers especially must focus on what takes place (or doesn't take place) in the classroom. Although there is no one right way to teach all students, empirically proven ways exist for increasing student performance through the implementation of direct and effective instructional strategies and tactics (cf. Algozzine et al., 1997).

A final note: Remember the copy machine scenario? Well, that special teacher's ninth-grade algebra class took the state-mandated end-of-course test, and 12 of 16 students passed! It's amazing what can happen when components of effective instruction provide guiding principles for the strategies and tactics used in teaching all students.

TEST YOUR KNOWLEDGE

Show what you know and learned in this chapter by answering the following questions. It's open book, so look back if you need to.

1. One of the earliest pushes to investigate accountability and student learning came from the _____ _____.

2. An unanticipated outcome of the creation of special education is a _____ system of educating students.

3. _____ _____ connected to standards, curriculum frameworks, and aligned assessment is vital to maximizing the performance of all students, including students with disabilities.

4. One of the purposes of an assessment is to remove the focus from solely on the _____ to that of what happens in the instructional environment.

5. We are educating students in an educational system where _____ is the constant and _____ is the variable.

6. There is a research-based model of effective instruction that has the following four components: _____, _____, _____, _____.

7. _____ for instruction is the backbone of effective instruction.

8. Evidence suggests that students often spend more time in _____ than engaged in learning.

9. _____ feeds the instructional process.

10. We can only blame the _____ for so long; then we must direct our attention to what matters: instruction.

ANSWERS

1. business community (p. 118)

2. dual, separate (p. 119)

3. Effective instruction (p. 119)

4. time, learning (p. 121)

5. student (p. 123)

6. planning, managing, delivering, evaluating (p. 125)

7. Planning (p. 126)

8. transition (p. 131)

9. Evaluation (p. 136)

10. assessment or test (p. 140)

REFLECTIONS ON CHANGE

See Appendix A for the Reflections on Change activity for this chapter (p. 192).

RECOMMENDED RESOURCES

Algozzine, B., Ysseldyke, J., & Elliott, J. (1997). *Strategies and tactics for effective instruction* (2d ed.). Longmont: CO, Sopris West.

Elliott, J., Algozzine, B., & Ysseldyke, J. (1998). *Timesavers for educators.* Longmont: CO, Sopris West.

Elmore, R. F., & Rothman, R. (Eds.) (1999). *Testing, teaching, and learning: A guide for states and school districts* (National Research Council report). Washington, DC: National Academy Press.

Levine, D. U., & Lazotte, L. W. (1990). *Unusually effective schools: A review and analysis of research and practice.* Madison, WI: National Center for Effective Schools.

Schumm, J. S., Vaughn, S., & Leavell, A. (1994). Planning pyramid: A framework for planning for diverse student needs during content area instruction. *The Reading Teacher, 47*(8), 608–615.

INTERNET RESOURCES

National Center to Improve the Tools of Educators (NCITE): http://idea.uoregon.edu/-ncite.
Sopris West, Inc.: www.sopriswest.com.

Improving Performance on Alternate Assessments Through Instruction

All of us do not have equal talent, but all of us should have an equal opportunity to develop our talent.

—John F. Kennedy

Good teaching is good teaching. There are no boundaries.

—Bob Algozzine

Hot-Button Issues

- Why did policymakers force us to have an alternate assessment that requires us to teach something that looks like academics to students who don't need academics?
- Can all students who have significant cognitive disabilities really learn?
- What in the heck does academic instruction look like for students who are in the alternate assessment?
- Does this type of instruction make any difference in these students' lives? In other words, is there any proof that this is worth it?

When we wrote the first edition of this book, it was the first year that states were required to have their alternate assessments in place. Thus most of our attention was on what the assessments were like—what their form and focus were. It is now four years later, and much has happened. Certainly a great deal more will still happen in the evolution of alternate assessments, but we are now at a point where we can step back from simply looking at what alternate assessments are to really look at what is happening—and should be happening—instructionally for students who are assessed through alternate assessments.

In this chapter, we first explore (but only briefly) the current status of alternate assessments. We clarify that we are focusing here on only those alternate assessments intended for students with significant cognitive disabilities—not those alternate assessments that are based on the same grade-level achievement standards as the general assessment (these were introduced in regulation by the No Child Left Behind [NCLB] Act in December 2003), or those alternate assessments based on modified achievement standards in pending NCLB regulations at the time the book was written. In our brief status review, we note primarily how alternate assessments have changed from when they were first conceptualized in 1997 in the Individuals With Disabilities Education Act (IDEA 97) to what they are now with the influence of NCLB and its accountability requirements. Then we devote the bulk of the chapter to a discussion of standards of learning for students in the alternate assessment, expectations held for these students, typical and research-based approaches to instruction, and examples of a curriculum for students who participate in the alternate. The information in this chapter represents a sea change from the kind of instruction that many have experienced in providing education to students with the most significant cognitive disabilities in the past.

FEDERAL REQUIREMENTS THAT GUIDE ALTERNATE ASSESSMENTS

Alternate assessments for students with significant cognitive disabilities have changed a lot since their inception in 1997. And they will continue to change a bit as states' understandings of the requirements from the U.S. Department of Education are clarified. In turn, what is implemented at the local level will slowly change as well. There are volumes of documents written by federal offices about alternate assessments. Despite the fact that this assessment is intended for a very small percentage of students, it has commanded considerable federal attention and time devoted to it in the form of regulation and guidance. These regulations and guidance documents come from both the Office of Special Education Programs and the Office of Elementary and Secondary Education (see Box 8.1 for documents), because the alternate assessment became important for special education and for Title I. But why so much attention? Probably it is because this assessment encompasses a group of students who in the past had pretty much been ignored. Until IDEA 97, these students were out of the large-scale assessment data picture completely (unless you were in Kentucky or perhaps Maryland).

Federal law (IDEA 97) indicated that alternate assessments are large-scale assessments for students who are unable to participate in general state assessments even with accommodations. These assessments provide a way for students with the most significant cognitive disabilities to participate in state assessments and to be included in accountability systems. Inclusion in

Box 8.1

Federal Documents That Clarify Alternate Assessments

Peer Review Guidance: Provides all the details of what the federal office of elementary and secondary education is looking for in the standards assessments for Title I (see www.ed .gov/policy/elsec/guid/saaprguidance/doc). For a checklist developed by Mid-South Regional Resource Center (MSRRC) and a short form tool for the Peer Review Guidance, check out the following:

MSRRC. (2004). *State standards and assessments: Critical elements checklist. Extracted from standards and assessments peer review guidance: Information and examples for meeting the requirements of NCLB* (April 28, 2004). www.ihdi.uky.edu/msrrc/

December 9, 2003, Regulations: Includes the specific regulation and rational for the alternate assessment based on alternate achievement standards and the reference to grade-level achievement standards. This document indicates that up to 1% of students with significant cognitive disabilities held to alternate achievement standards may be considered proficient for NCLB. Available on the main NCLB Web site: www.ed.gov/nclb

Guidance for December 9, 2003, Regulations: Provides details on what the federal Office of Elementary and Secondary Education is looking for in the alternate assessments, both those based on grade-level achievement standards and those based on alternate achievement standards (not yet released when this book was written).

Pending Regulation: Will include the specific regulation and rationale for the alternate assessment based on modified achievement standards. It will most likely indicate the percentage of students (up to 2%) who can be considered proficient for NCLB based on modified achievement standards.

accountability is a key element of NCLB. A special federal regulation was created to ensure that the performance of students with the most significant cognitive disabilities was recognized and counted, even though the performance of these students looked different from the performance of students taking the general assessment. And the performance of these students could be deemed "proficient" just as any other students' performance if the state had followed a rigorous set of procedures to define what was "proficient" for the group of students with significant cognitive disabilities.

Additional regulations further clarified that alternate assessments were to be based on academic content standards. Henceforth, the creation of alternate assessments based on alternate achievement standards and alternate assessments based on grade-level achievement standards, and pending NCLB regulations at the time this book was written, introduced alternate assessment based on modified achievement standards.

How these assessments reflect the depth and breadth of the grade-level content depends on whether the alternate assessment is based on alternate achievement standards or grade-level achievement standards. For alternate assessments based on grade-level achievement standards, the depth and breadth of assessed content should be the same as on the general assessment in order to draw accurate inferences about student proficiency. Alternate assessments based on alternate achievement standards must also assess student achievement on the grade-level content. However, the performance standards will differ.

Alternate Assessments Based on Alternate Achievement Standards. Some students with significant cognitive disabilities can be assessed using alternate formats aligned to the grade-level content, but based on alternate achievement standards that define proficiency differently from the general assessment. Students who participate in this assessment are those who require substantial modifications, adaptations, or supports to meaningfully access the grade-level content or who require intensive individualized instruction to acquire and generalize knowledge. Additionally, these students are those who are unable to demonstrate achievement of academic content standards on a paper-and-pencil test, even with accommodations.

Alternate Assessments Based on Grade-Level Achievement Standards. Other students with disabilities, not necessarily those with significant cognitive disabilities, may require alternate formats aligned to grade-level content that is based on grade-level achievement standards, or the same definition of proficiency as the general assessment. This approach to alternate assessment was formerly or commonly known as alternative assessment. That is, alternative assessments were known to test the same content and used the same performance standards, but the means and methods of assessment were different. Students who participate in this alternate grade-level assessment are those able to achieve grade-level achievement standards via different assessments or contexts than are traditionally provided.

Recent federal laws and regulations have forced many states that had earlier identified one set of prioritized content standards across all grade levels for their alternate assessment to now align to grade-level content. This reflects NCLB regulations and guidance requirements that all assessments must be aligned to the grade-level content for the enrolled grade of the student being assessed.

The federal requirements have also used a lot of terms in new and unique ways. The term "achievement standards" was used instead of the formerly familiar term "performance standards." Even with that, many educators confused *achievement* and *academic*, perhaps thinking content standards when they should have been thinking performance standards—or was that the other way around? Be assured that there has been much confusion that goes back to the word that is being currently used. Box 8.2 contains some of the basic terms that are being used in relation to alternate assessments with a brief and basic definition of each. It is wise to refer to these often to be sure you are using the terms correctly.

The 1% Cap. There is another critical piece of information that was thrown into the mix of federal requirements under NCLB that confused a lot of people—namely, the 1% cap. This requirement was for accountability purposes and closing loopholes of who and how many participated in what assessment.

Box 8.2

Definitions of Basic Terms Used in Relation to Alternate Assessments

Achievement Standards: "How well" students are to perform to achieve the content standards; previously referred to as performance standards; when setting standards, questions were asked about what is considered "adequate" or "world-class" performance; an implicit assumption is that the performance is grade-level based for students in the general assessment.

Alternate Achievement Standards: "How well" students are to achieve the content standards based on a set of criteria that is qualitatively different so it addresses the characteristics of students with significant cognitive disabilities.

Content Standards: What students should know and be able to do. Most states have these in a variety of areas, primarily academic, but also often in art, physical education, and other areas as well. No Child Left Behind focuses on reading, mathematics, and science content standards.

Grade-Level Achievement Standards: "How well" students are to achieve the content standards based on criteria that are based on grade-level performance standards; this language was introduced in the December 9 NCLB Regulations to clarify that some students with disabilities might participate in an alternate assessment that was based on grade-level achievement standards; these would be *in contrast to* students with significant cognitive disabilities assessed through alternate assessments based on alternate achievement standards.

Modified Achievement Standards: "How well" students are to achieve the content standards based on criteria that are probably between alternate achievement standards and grade level achievement standards. These will be defined in a regulation not yet published at the time this book was written.

The 1% cap basically says that there is no limitation on how many students with disabilities can participate in alternate assessments. What it also says is that there is a limit of 1% of the total alternate assessment scores that can be counted as proficient and above and reported at the district and state levels. Without this 1% cap there was concern that districts or states might find it tempting to place many students with disabilities, namely, those with less or no significant cognitive disabilities, in the alternate assessments and have them held to the alternate achievement standards (which might be perceived as easier). This cap is not applied to the school level because it is recognized that there are school-based programs that may serve a higher prevalence of students with significant cognitive disabilities at one particular site than others, thereby having a higher percentage of these students by default. In other words, these sites would start with more than 1% of students with significant cognitive disabilities simply based on how the students are assigned to schools. Therefore, it would be unfair to hold these particular sites to the 1% cap.

Although intended to curb the overuse of alternate assessments, the 1% cap has caused much confusion. For example, in some cases there have been very low levels of participation of students in alternate assessment because there were those who assumed that it was 1% of all students with disabilities, rather than of *all* students. In fact 1% of all students is about 9–10% of students with disabilities; the actual percentage depends on the actual prevalence of students with disabilities.

What We Knew Then

In 1997, when the concept of alternate assessment was put into law, states attempted to identify what would be assessed on them. Some camps argued that these students should be assessed according to what was written on their Individualized Education Programs (IEPs). Other camps argued for developmental task analysis type of assessment activities. Yet others argued for a broad set or expanded set of standards to be identified on which students would be assessed. A heavier emphasis was placed on efforts to identify a separate set of standards or even the same standards, but different performance indicators. As the journey of alternate assessments began, so, too, did the varied paths states took to find their way according to their state's constituent groups, stakeholders, and advisory boards. The way to developing alternate assessments focused on four general approaches—observation, interviews and checklists, testing, and record review (see Thurlow, Elliott, & Ysseldyke, 2003, for a detailed review of alternate assessments). Criteria for who should take the alternate assessment were developed. The issues surrounding how and where to report the results loomed large. How would the scores of students who took the alternate assessment count in accountability systems? Would they count at all?

Where We Are Now

What do alternate assessments look like now after all these new regulations and clarifications? It is important to recognize that they are still evolving, even seven years after IDEA 97. With that in mind, and with the new reauthorization of the Individuals With Disabilities Education Improvement Act of 2004 (IDEA 2004), a specific description of what states are currently doing would be rather meaningless. Instead, we have decided to give a general sense of where states are now.

To some extent, states' alternate assessments based on alternate achievement standards have reflected the evolution that we have seen in our education of students with significant cognitive disabilities. That is, movement from sole emphasis on developmental tasks and goals to emphasis on academic content standards. When states first began creating alternate assessments, many of them were developmental in nature, reflecting an emphasis on the goals of early development, whether academic or behavioral. Some had these students involved in lower grade-level standards. Others included students in curriculum, but with no expectations for learning. Yet others had content involvement with no curriculum, and others had students learning an entirely different curriculum altogether. As educators began to realize that students could do things beyond the developmental tasks on which they were working, the shift to an emphasis on standards-based educational goals for students with significant cognitive disabilities started. In many ways, the birth of functional academics was an attempt to bridge developmental and functional skills to academic ones. The emphasis of nearly all states' alternate assessments now clearly is on academic goals. It is our belief that this shift from developmental to functional and academic standards is a result of the elevated emphasis on inclusive assessment and accountability for all students, including those with the most significant cognitive disabilities.

Current forms of states' alternate assessments primarily focus on *collections of evidence.* Several states use some type of *performance assessment,* which are more direct measures of students' skills. Other states use *checklists,* in which an observer marks student performance or a teacher remembers the students' skills and marks them.

A final area of continued development of states' alternate assessment has to do with the actual administration. Who collects the data? Who scores the data? How much training is provided to teachers and others before the alternate assessment begins? Whether the alternate assessment is a yearlong endeavor or an event that takes place during the same testing window as the general assessment, these are all variables on which states' alternate assessments vary still today. Keep in mind that these alternate assessment variations reflect differences in states' approaches that are similar, if not the same, as the variations in the regular state assessments.

As far as reporting goes, all students and their assessment results count and are accounted for! This includes students in the alternate assessment based on alternate achievement standards.

What Has Changed

We think it is probably pretty clear to you by now—by "it," we mean all the changes and metamorphoses of policies, regulations, practices, and even attitudes toward educating and accounting for all students with disabilities, including those with significant disabilities. To name just a few, there are high standards for all students, high expectations for all students, grade-level content standards for all students, accountability for all students, reporting results for all students, and including alternate assessments. Perhaps the most far-reaching impact the alternate assessment has had on the field of special education is that of instruction for the students with the most significant cognitive disabilities.

High Standards for Learning
for Alternate Assessment Students

As we mentioned earlier, there has been a shift, or even abandonment, of the developmental approach to instruction for students with significant cognitive disabilities. In the past, students with significant cognitive disabilities received instruction on lower grade-level content, yet there was no adherence to the intent of the standards being taught. In the past, students received instruction on the same grade-level content standards and curriculum, but the focus was on prerequisite skills instead of adhering to the intent of the standards. In the past, students worked solely on access skills such as motor, social, and communication within the context of grade-level curricular activities.

Most instruction of these students had focused on age-appropriate activities with no expectations for learning the required skills, concepts, or knowledge of any particular standard. Students primarily worked on learning access skills within age-appropriate activities but, sadly, not grade-level curriculum activities. It was these instructional practices that kept students working primarily on developmental progression skills that were based in prekindergarten and early elementary levels. It is these same practices that exposed students to socially invalid activities when compared to same-aged peers.

In reality, we have missed the instructional target for these students for many reasons. One is the fact that developmental or functional curriculum is the tradition in serving these students. Another is that there has been a general lack of understanding of academic standards by special educators. And finally, the lack of access to and understanding of assistive technology has also had an impact.

THE IMPACT OF ALTERNATE ASSESSMENT ON INSTRUCTION

It is easy to say that we must hold high expectations for all students. It is easy to believe that we are holding high expectations for students. But the alternate assessment for students with significant cognitive disabilities has begun to open up expectations in ways that few policy requirements have in the past. The alternate assessment, to some extent, has forced us to look at students in ways that we have not looked at them before.

We have now started to hear some of the early implementers of alternate assessments wonder aloud whether their expectations for their students with significant cognitive disabilities were too low. We have heard this statement made by states that developed portfolio assessments and states that developed performance assessments. Although there has been little research that has looked at expectations for students with the most significant cognitive disabilities, it is likely that what we have learned is that expectations have their greatest effects on the lowest performing students. To the surprise of many, the effects of these low expectations do impact those students who are often thought of as the least likely to be affected.

There is now much literature to be read and reviewed that eloquently lays out how developmental approaches have not worked and in fact have shortchanged students (for a discussion, see Browder, 2001, 2003; Kleinert & Kearns, 2004). We will give you a hint—happily we are all reaching an understanding of how access to the general academic curriculum and its grade-level content is essential! There are some who worry that this focus will mean that we lose the use of functional skills that these students very much need. Not to worry, because the best practice approach to this is to merge the two. How you go about doing that is critical. One must start at the content standards first. Using grade-level curriculum and high expectations for performance will no doubt land you on the alignment of instruction and standards that the law requires.

Hitting the Target. One way to hit the instructional alignment target is to be sure students with significant cognitive disabilities receive instruction on grade-level content standards, which may be at a lower level of complexity, within the context of grade-level curriculum. By doing this, you will ensure that the grade-level standards remain in tact. Further, to gain access to this grade-level content, use the same instructional materials, adapted versions of the materials, or appropriate assistive technology to provide curricular access. All curriculum planning should adhere to the principles of universal design, including (1) considering the widest array of possible users of the curriculum, (2) representing curricular material through multiple means, (3) using multiple means of expression or representation of thought, and (4) providing a variety of means of engagement.

It helps to look at a few state standards and examine how states have tried to pull out the intent or essence of those standards, that is, still keeping them at grade level so that students with significant cognitive disabilities have access to grade-level content standards. Box 8.3 gives an example of some content standards in Massachusetts and their essence for students with significant cognitive disabilities, as well for measurement in the alternate assessment. Other states have approached this task in a similar manner, sometimes referring to extended standards or expanded standards as links to the content standards. Even though a standard is described in terms of its essence, or it is expanded to apply to students with significant cognitive disabilities, it is still based on the grade-level standard.

Educators working with students with significant cognitive disabilities should keep in mind the critical importance of targeting the grade-level content standards for each and every student. Figuring out how to do just that is the trick. Massachusetts has given great thought to points of access to the grade-level content. The state has identified less complex points of access and more complex points of access, and it has included instructional ideas for the points of access. If your state or district has not provided information to help you identify how to give your students with significant cognitive disabilities access to grade-level content standards, checking out the Massachusetts model will be helpful. (Don't forget to look at the Web site as well.) Box 8.4 shows an example of an Instructional Idea (based on Learning Standards), and the ways in which students can participate in an activity.

Other approaches have identified considerations to keep in mind or steps to follow with individual students. Research in Kentucky had found that the scores of students on the alternate assessment were related to the extent to which teachers embedded the portfolio alternate assessment into their ongoing instructional activities (see Chapter 5 for a thorough discussion of this). By doing this, teachers made each student an active participant in the development of their portfolio. Kleinert and Kearns (2004) have suggested that a way to merge instruction and assessment of portfolio or body-of-evidence alternate assessments is to use these steps:

Step 1: Define the outcome of instruction.

Step 2: Link to the appropriate standards.

Step 3: Identify instructional activities and how the student will participate.

Step 4: Target IEP objective most aligned with the activity.

Box 8.3

Example of Standards of Learning for Alternate Assessments in Massachusetts

Mathematics

Strand 1

Number Sense & Operations

7–8

CONTENT   Mathematics

STRAND   Number Sense & Operations

Grade Level 7–8			
Learning Standards as written		*Essence of the Standard(s)*	
Number Sense	8.N.1	Compare, order, estimate, and translate among integers, fractions and mixed numbers (i.e., rational numbers), decimals, and percents.	• Use a variety of numerical forms, including whole, prime, rational, and irrational numbers
	8.N.2	Define, compare, order, and apply frequently used irrational numbers, such as the square root of 2 and pi.	• Continue to use relationships between numbers (whole numbers, fractions, decimals, percents, integers, rational, irrational)
	8.N.3	Use ratios and proportions in the solution of problems, in particular, problems involving unit rates, scale factors, and rate of change.	
	8.N.4	Represent numbers in scientific notation, and use them in calculations and problem situations.	• Use proportional relationships and rate of change to solve problems
	8.N.5	Apply number theory concepts, including prime factorization and relatively prime numbers, to the solution of problems.	

Operations	8.N.6	Demonstrate an understanding of absolute value, e.g. $|-3| = |3|$	• Use computation skills to simplify equations, using fractions, rules of powers/roots, real numbers
	8.N.7	Apply the rules of powers and roots to the solution of problems. Extend the order of operations to include positive integer exponents and square roots.	• Extend the Order of Operations (positive integer exponents and square roots)
	8.N.8	Demonstrate an understanding of the properties of arithmetic operations on rational numbers. Use the associative, communicative, and distributive properties; properties of the identity and inverse elements (e.g., $-7 + 7 = 0$; $3/4 \times 4/3 = 1$); and the notion of closure of a subset of the rational numbers under an operation (e.g., the set of odd integers is closed under multiplication but not under addition).	• Solve problems with accuracy, efficiency, and simplicity
	8.N.12	Select and use appropriate operations—addition, subtraction, multiplication, division, and positive integer exponents—to solve problems with rational numbers (including negatives).	

SOURCE: Massachusetts Department of Education. (Fall, 2001). *MCAS alternate assessment: Resource guide to the Massachusetts curriculum frameworks for students with significant disabilities: Mathematics* (p. 138). Malden, MA: Author.

Step 5: Select documentation of learning and instruction.

Step 6: Organize the documentation of learning and instruction.

(Kleinert & Kearns, 2004, pp. 139–142)

Box 8.4

Example of Instructional Idea, Strategies, and Entry Points in Massachusetts

Instructional Idea (Based on Learning Standards 8.N.1, 8.N.10, and 8.N.12)

At grades 7–8 (or an equivalent age), students are told they have a bank account of $10,000 with which to purchase stocks from the New York Stock Exchange. They research a variety of stocks and make selections for purchase. Each day, the students keep track of the percentage each stock rises/falls and answer questions involving percentages when given projections about their stocks (e.g., on Day 1, Stock #1 rises 50% in value; on Day 2, it falls 50% in value; on Day 3, it rises 50%; on Day 4, it falls 50%. How much—to the nearest penny— is it worth at the end of Day 4?). Students keep track of the percentage lost or gained per stock, as well as the total amount of money lost or gained.

How All Students Can Participate in This Activity

Addressing Learning Standard(s) as Written for This Grade Level	*Possible Assessment Strategies and Portfolio Products*
Paul keeps track of his stock portfolio. He uses stock quotes in the paper to record daily changes and make written observations. He solves related problems using knowledge of percents.	• Paul's research on various stocks, paired with an explanation of his choices • Paul's stock portfolio with calculations • Paul's written review and reflection of the activity • Paul's graph of grades earned during this unit on percents
Addressing Learning Standard(s) at Lower Levels of Complexity ("entry points")	*Possible Assessment Strategies and Portfolio Products*
Nadia participates in a similar activity using percents. She identifies items for purchase from newspaper flyers. She solves problems related to percent discount using a table (percents to decimal) and a calculator.	• Data on Nadia's independence in performing simple calculations involving percents using her table and calculator • Nadia's table of percent-to-decimal conversions • Videotape of Nadia using her visual and calculator to solve a problem • Nadia's reflection sheet and graph of her performance of this task on several occasions
Addressing Access Skill(s) (skills embedded in academic instruction)	*Possible Assessment Strategies and Portfolio Products*
Greg helps his peers research different stocks. He uses the computer, Braille keyboard, and IntelliKeys overlays to locate information related to this activity.	• Data collected on Greg's ability to locate information in Braille • Peer note describing Greg's participation in the activity • Photographs of Greg using Braille in a variety of settings (working at his weekend journal at home, typing his name in school, using IntelliKeys overlays paired with Braille to participate in a science experiment, etc.)

SOURCE: Massachusetts Department of Education. (Fall, 2001). *MCAS alternate assessment: Resource guide to the Massachusetts curriculum frameworks for students with significant disabilities: Mathematics* (p. 140). Malden, MA: Author.

Regardless of the approach of connecting instruction to the content standards, the critical element is to ensure that the connection is made to the academic content. Again, this does not mean we throw out all things functional—certainly not, for we know that students with significant cognitive disabilities still need functional skills (not unlike many other students!). Integrating the two and working on both is the best approach. And, maintaining a focus on academics is essential.

Approaches to Instruction. Finding grade-level standards-based approaches to instruction for students with significant cognitive disabilities can present a challenge. In fact, these practices as a whole are still emerging. One of the best sources is your state's or district's curriculum frameworks and training materials. If your state or district has not developed them, look to other states that have assumed a grade-level approach for students with significant cognitive disabilities. But first, be sure that it is starting from the basic foundation of the same content standards applied to all students. Figuring out exactly which states those are is like aiming at a moving target. Dr. Margaret McLaughlin, a longtime leader in helping the field address access issues, has remarked on the importance of keeping several principles in mind when thinking about access to the general curriculum and what it looks like at grade level. She indicates that it is a collaborative planning process among parents, students, and teachers. It involves the following four activities:

1. Defining critical knowledge and performance expectations in the general curriculum

2. Identifying aids, supports, and services necessary

3. Reflecting longitudinal views of learning

4. Integrating and aligning content and instruction

The same principles should apply to all students with disabilities as they receive standards-based grade-level academic instruction.

As we progress in our understanding of alternate assessments and grade-level alignment, we will most certainly improve our understanding of what instruction must look and sound like to ensure that students with significant cognitive disabilities reach those standards. The Long Beach Unified School District (LBUSD) has started down the road to this end. It has developed course outlines for students with significant cognitive disabilities, something that less than a decade ago was almost unheard of. Box 8.5 provides pages from just one of many LBUSD Board of Education–approved course outlines for high school course content that are available to ensure that students with significant cognitive disabilities have access to and achieve success in these content standard areas. Similar course outlines have been developed for other students with disabilities (see Recommended Resources for Web site). It is this district's belief that students with significant cognitive disabilities should be taught skills that will enhance students' independence in skills of daily living, that they should be taught academic content because it is functional and socially valid, and that they should be presumed competent and not denied instruction offered to students of the same age.

Box 8.5

Selections From a Functional High School Course Outline

Office of Curriculum, Instruction, and Professional Development

Special Education Course Outline

Department: Special Education   Course Title: Functional Academics/English/LA MS SDC

Course Code: 5430   Grade Level: 6–12   Course Length: 1 year   Credits/Semester: 5

Required for Graduation: No Meets H.S. Graduation Requirement: Yes   Elective Credit: Yes

Prerequisites: IEP placement in a M/S classroom

Course Description:

This course provides functional language arts skills to students in the moderate to severe Special Day Classroom (SDC); students are both English only background and English language learners. Reading instruction includes oral language development, as well as concepts about print, phonics, sight reading, and vocabulary. Students also learn reading skills from a selected reading program. They will learn to identify and use functional words in the community. Students will learn basic writing skills to extend their learning beyond the IEP. Students will be encouraged to use a variety of modes of communication including, but not limited to, rebus, sign, oral, written, picture-based communication, vocal output devices, computer programs, and other forms familiar to the students. Activities and topics covered in English Language Arts (ELA) may be contained in the California Alternate Performance Assessment (CAPA) and are included in California's Content Standards for English Language Arts and English Language Development (ELD).

The goal of the Long Beach Unified School District (LBUSD) is to enable students identified as individuals with exceptional needs to improve their skills in functional academics so that they can function as independently as possible at home, at school, in a vocational setting, and in community. This course of study is designed to meet the individual needs of the student as indicated on his or her IEP and, in addition, extend student learning beyond the IEP.

Goals:

Students will:

- Respond to or use a form of communication in natural settings, or both.
- Construct meaning from connected text (English or home language).
- Read functional words, phrases, and so on.
- Locate information by using a variety of consumer, workplace, and public documents.
- Using writing to communicate in English and in the primary language.

California Alternate Performance Assessment (CAPA)

English Language Arts Standards:

Note: ELD standards, matched to ELA standards and differentiated by level of English proficiency, should be used with English learners for listening, speaking, reading, and writing.

ELA/CAPA Standard 1

Reading Word Analysis

- Read simple one-syllable and high-frequency words (i.e., sight words).
- Recognize and name all uppercase and lowercase letters of the alphabet.
- Match all consonant and short-vowel sounds to appropriate letters.
- Understand that printed materials provide information.
- Match oral words to printed words.
- Identify letters, words, and sentences.
- Classify grade-appropriate categories of words (i.e., concrete collections of animals, foods, toys).
- Recognize common abbreviations (i.e., Jan., Sun., Mr., St.).

ELA/CAPA Standard 2

Reading/Reading Comprehension

- Follow one- and two-step written instructions.
- Ask and answer questions about essential elements of a text.
- Identify the main events of the plot, their causes, and the influence of each event on future events.
- Identify the structural features of popular media (i.e., newspapers, magazines, online information) and use the features to obtain information.
- Locate information by using a variety of consumer, workplace, and public documents.

ELA/CAPA Standard 3

Writing/Writing Strategies

- Write by moving from left to right and from top to bottom.
- Print legibly and space letters, words, and sentences appropriately.
- Demonstrate basic keyboarding skills and familiarity with computer technology (i.e., cursor, software, memory disk drive, hard drive).

ELA/CAPA Standard 4

Listening and Speaking/Listening and Speaking Strategies

- Understand and follow one- and two-step oral directions.
- Listen attentively.
- Share information and ideas, speaking audibly in complete, coherent sentences.
- Give, restate, and follow simple two-step directions.
- Stay on the topic when speaking.
- Ask questions for clarification and understanding.
- Recount experiences in a logical sequence.

ELA/CAPA Standard 5

Listening and Speaking/Speaking Applications

- Describe people, places, things (i.e., size, color, shape), locations, and actions.
- Apply appropriate interview techniques.

(Continued)

(Continued)

Performance Objectives Addressing ELA CAPA Standards

Upon completion of this course of study, and according to individual ability levels and Individual Education Program goals, the student will:

Listening

- Listen to a passage and answer questions.
- Listen attentively during instruction (i.e., directions and direct instruction, read aloud).

Speaking/Communication (English or primary language)

- Communicate with language (i.e., oral, alternative communication, nonverbal).
- Expand language to communicate about things unrelated to self.
- Join his or her language to the language of others in conversation.
- Respond to and use language for a variety of purposes.
- Respond to and use increasingly complex language structure correctly.
- Share ideas.
- Speak and communicate in complete and coherent sentences.
- Listen to the school or class bulletin and plan a daily or weekly schedule.
- Report on a current event after listening to a newscast.
- Answer or give input during instruction (i.e., read-alouds, direct instruction).
- Stay on topic when speaking.
- Give, restate, and follow two-step directions.
- Use words, phrases, or complete sentences to tell a story.
- Ask questions for clarification and understanding.
- Ask questions about text at the end of the story.
- Recount experiences in a logical sequence.
- Use appropriate language for interviewing.
- Describe people, places, things, locations, and actions.
- Recite personal information.

Emergent Reading

- Concepts about print (English or primary language)
    Hold a book correctly.
    Know that printed material provides information.
    Turn pages correctly.
    Look at pictures/pages left to right.
    Identify the starting point on a page of print.
    Identify letters, words, and sentences.
    Track words left to right.
    Track words with one-to-one correspondence.
    Show an understanding of return sweep.
    Identify the front, back, and spine of a book.

- Recognize and identify colors.
- Recognize and identify shapes.
- Classify categories of words and pictures.
- Recognize, match, and identify all upper- and lowercase letters of the alphabet.

- Show an interest in books by looking, listening, reading, and participating in a shared reading experience.
- Match pictures.
- Decode words.
- Encode words.

Early Reading (English or primary language)

- Use LBUSD core literature reading material for listening, reading, and writing.
- Use illustrations and language patterns to begin to read transitional text (i.e., pattern books).
- Read simple one-syllable words and use them as anchors in text.
- Read first 200 high-frequency words.
- Match all consonant and short-vowel sounds to appropriate letters.
- Match oral words to printed words.
- Identify the sound of each letter of the alphabet.
- Identify and present personal information.
- Identify LBUSD protective vocabulary and apply it.
- Identify job application terms and fill out a job application.
- Identify frequently used words.
- Recognize common abbreviations.
- Find a book written at all the students' instructional level at the school or public library.
- Read a simple recipe in a cookbook.
- Utilize a bus schedule.
- Identify the organizational features of popular media (i.e., newspapers, internet, TV, magazines, catalogues) and use the features to obtain information about current events, weather, shopping (i.e., sales), and entertainment.

Reading Comprehension (English or primary language)

- Use pictures and personal knowledge to make predictions about text.
- Follow one-step written directions.
- Follow two-step written directions.
- Ask and answer questions about essential elements of a text.
- Identify main events of the plot, their causes, and the influence of each event on future events.
- Retell a story.
- Sequence events in a text.

Writing (English or primary language)

- Dictate simple sentences.
- Generate a one- or two-sentence story for writing.
- Hold a marker.
- Hold a pencil.
- Mark on paper.
- Use a pencil to trace lines, shapes, or letters.
- Use a pencil to copy lines, shapes, or letters (with and without a model).

(Continued)

(Continued)

- Write or print by moving from left to right and from top to bottom.
- Write or print upper- and lowercase letters.
- Write or print legibly and space letters, words, and sentences appropriately.
- Trace, copy, and write personal information.
- Copy and write simple sentences.
- Know basic computer terminology (i.e., mouse, keyboard, screen, etc.).
- Keyboard individual letters.
- Keyboard personal information.
- Keyboard simple sentences.
- Use technology to generate writing exercises.
- Complete an application (i.e., California Identification Card, public library card, employment application).
- Participate in shared writing experience.
- Maintain an interactive journal with teacher or aide.

Outline of Content and Time Allotment

Functional academics should be taught one period daily or one block. Each topic for instruction should be covered every year by integrating and revisiting related topics recursively.

Outline of Content:

- Alphabet.
- Phonics.
- Identify and write LBUSD protective vocabulary.
- Identify LBUSD job application terms and vocabulary.
- Fill out job applications.
- Learn and identify frequently used words (i.e., Dolch word list).

Or:

The teacher may teach the various performance objectives throughout the year on a continual basis as they relate to the content or monthly theme. For example, a teacher may teach safety in November; however, the protective vocabulary is paced to teach later in the year. The teacher has flexibility to teach the safety unit on the condition that the performance objectives in this course outline are used to drive the instruction.

Community-Based Instruction (CBI):

Due to the difficulty M/S students have in generalizing and transferring learning, it is imperative that students practice their speaking, reading, and writing skills in the environments in which they will be using them. Community-based instruction becomes an invaluable tool for assisting the student with a severe cognitive impairment to learn, retain, and master the skills needed to become an effective listener, reader, and communicator.

Assistive Technology (AT) and Augmentative/Alternative Communication (AAC):

Assistive technology (AT) and augmentative/alternative communication (AAC) devices and materials that have been assigned to the student through IEP documentation need to be integrated into the program whenever possible or appropriate.

SOURCE: Excerpt from the Long Beach Unified School District, Office of Curriculum, Instruction, and Professional Development. (2004). *High school course outline: Functional academics, ELA* (pp. 1–5).

SUMMARY

In this chapter we presented information on alternate assessments and how to begin to transform instruction so that it is aligned to standards-based, grade-level academic content standards. This is truly a time of transformation—and a time of challenge as well. If you are in a state where the transformation has not yet occurred, it will take extra stamina to figure out how to integrate grade-level academic standards into otherwise functional or developmental materials. It can be done, and your students will benefit even though it is not the ideal way to go about it.

Alternate assessments have come into their own with NCLB, which has given them a role in accountability, allowing students with significant cognitive disabilities to have alternate achievement standards for proficiency. With these incentives, knowing the content standards and providing good instruction become more important. Several researchers have provided ideas for what good instruction looks like for students with significant cognitive disabilities—these ideas generally include knowing the content standards, aligning instruction to those standards, and relating these to the students' IEP and needed accommodations and modifications. Assistive technology is frequently mentioned in examples of how learning is accomplished. Expectations are also usually a part of the picture.

TEST YOUR KNOWLEDGE

Take a peek at this little assessment and show what you know.

1. Alternate assessments provide a way for students with the most significant _____ disabilities to participate in state assessments and to be included in accountability.

2. The 1% cap requirement was for _____ purposes. There are no limitations on how many students can participate in alternate assessments.

3. Achievement standards is the term used to refer to how well students are to performance to achieve the _____ _____.

4. The emphasis of all states' alternate assessments now clearly is on _____ goals.

5. Even though a standard might be described in terms of its essence, or it might be expanded to apply to students with significant cognitive disabilities, it still must be based on _____ content.

6. The _____ assessment has begun to open up expectations in ways that few policy requirements have in the past decade.

7. Connecting instruction to academic content standards does not mean we throw out all things _____.

8. The principles that Dr. Margaret McLaughlin has identified for access to the general education curriculum should apply to _____ students

with disabilities as they receive standards-based, grade-level academic instruction.

9. Besides research, the other place to go for guidance is existing curriculum frameworks and _____ material.

10. Alternate assessments have come into their own with _____, which allows students with significant cognitive disabilities to have alternate achievement standards for proficiency.

ANSWERS

1. cognitive (p. 144)

2. accountability (p. 146)

3. content standards (p. 147)

4. academic (p. 149)

5. alternate (p. 150)

6. grade-level (p. 151)

7. functional (p. 155)

8. all (p. 155)

9. training (p. 155)

10. NCLB (p. 161)

REFLECTIONS ON CHANGE

See Appendix A for the Reflections on Change activity for this chapter (p. 192).

RECOMMENDED RESOURCES

Browder, D. (2001). *Curriculum and assessment for students with moderate and severe disabilities.* New York: Guilford.

Browder, D. (2003). Consideration of what may influence student outcomes on alternate assessment. *Education and Training in Developmental Disabilities, 38*(3), 255–270.

Kleinert, H. L., & Kearns, J. F. (2004). Alternate assessments. In F. P. Orelove, D. S. Obsey, & R. K. Siberman (Eds.), *Educating children with multiple disabilities: A collaborative approach* (pp. 115-149). Baltimore: Paul H. Brookes.

Massachusetts Department of Education. (2001, Fall). *MCAS alternate assessment: Resource guide to the MA curriculum frameworks for students with significant disabilities, mathematics.* Malden, MA: Author.

Nolet, V., & McLaughlin, M. (2000). *Accessing the general curriculum: Including students with disabilities in standards-based reform.* Thousand Oaks, CA: Corwin.

INTERNET RESOURCES

Intellitools: www.intellitools.com
Long Beach Unified School District: www.lbusd.k12.ca.us
National Alternate Assessment Center (NAAC): www.naacpartners.org
National Center on Education Outcomes: www.nceo.info (see Alternate Assessments)
Universal Design for Learning: www.cast.org/udl

Parent Support for Student Performance

A stumble may prevent a fall.

—English proverb

As parents of children with and without disabilities, we expect to be active partners involved in all levels of educational decision making. We require quality, accountability, and proof that our children are learning from our public education systems.

—Debbie Johnson, Parent

Hot-Button Issues

- What do parents really need to know about testing? What can they do to help their child do better?
- Even if you let parents know what they can do to help their child perform better, they won't really do it.
- Giving parents too much information is dangerous; they will just have stuff to use in lawsuits.

Parents and families are important players in the attempt to improve student performance. Yet schools rarely capitalize on their potential, probably for many reasons. One reason may be that we don't trust parents to do what we think needs to be done. Another reason may be that some doubt they know enough to be able to do what needs to be done. And, perhaps more common yet, it takes time and effort to help parents understand what they can do to help improve student performance. Some educators are concerned that the time and effort devoted to parents takes away from the time and effort that we can devote directly to students. However, this time and effort almost always have significant benefits for students.

In this chapter, we show you the many ways that parents can indeed help improve the achievement and test performance of students with disabilities. First, we discuss the need to inform parents about testing. This includes presenting the reason for administering district and state tests as well as their characteristics (such as multiple-choice math questions, short-answer reading questions, and long-answer writing tasks). Next, we address the issues of who has the last say about whether a child takes a test and the responsibility of schools not to encourage inappropriate recommendations to parents about this decision.

We also address in this chapter the important topic of how to equip parents with the knowledge and resources to make good decisions about test participation and accommodations. Then we provide ways to help parents understand what test results mean, both in general and specifically in relation to how their child performed on the test.

In addition to the resources that we provide at the end of each chapter, we identify several resource centers for parents and other family members as well as specific materials that have been developed to inform parents about district and state assessments, accommodations, and a variety of related topics.

INFORMING PARENTS ABOUT TESTS

To help parents make good decisions and help them learn how to support their children so that the children can perform optimally, it is essential that they know about the test. This means that they need to know about the purpose of the test, the content areas tested, the types of items that are included on the test, how long the test or each part of the test usually takes, where and how the test is usually administered, and what the consequences of their children's performance on the test are.

We again recommend that you develop a test matrix. Start with the one developed in Chapter 4. This matrix may need to be simplified or rearranged for parents. Box 9.1 shows an example of a test matrix that was developed specifically for parents.

Another strategy that usually is helpful to parents, and in turn to their children, is to give parents a sample test. If your district or state releases items each year, then many possible items are available to you to use to develop a sample test for parents. Send it home to parents. Ask them to look the items over to see what their children will be doing when they take the test. Suggest that they try some of the items. Encourage them to work on some of the items with their children.

As an alternative, you could organize a parent test night. Give parents not only the opportunity to see what the test is like but also to discuss with other parents ways in which they can help their children perform well on the test. By bringing parents together in this way, you also increase the possibility of collaborative efforts by groups of parents. Sometimes these collaborative efforts result

Box 9.1

A Parent Version of a Test Matrix

Topic	# Items	Sample Item	What My Child Has to Do
Synonyms: Recognize a word that means the same as another word.	18 items	A filly is a kind of • turtle • rabbit • horse • frog	Your child will have to tell the difference between the correct word and one that is fairly close in meaning to it. The more you can help your child increase his or her vocabulary, the better, especially when you can note differences between words that are close in meaning to each other.
Multiple Meanings: Determine the meaning of a word that has multiple meanings.	6 items	I cannot bear to tell my mom I skipped school. In which sentence does the word *bear* mean the same thing as in the sentence above? • I saw a bear eating my picnic lunch. • The bridge will bear 10 tons. • My brother bears well in school. • He bears up well under pressure.	Your child will need to get the exact meaning of a word from the sentence in which it is used. Words that are pronounced the same but that have different meanings are what is being tested. The more you can highlight these for your child, the better.
Context: Pick the best word to use, given a sentence or paragraph.	6 items	Use the other words in the sentence to help you figure out what the underlined word means. After the earthquake, the dog dug through the *rubble* until he found his master. • yard • house • broken concrete • tunnel	Your child will need to pick out the best word just from having read a sentence in which a word meaning approximately the same thing is included. The more you can help your child increase his or her vocabulary, the better. Playing games in which your child guesses at the missing word is also helpful in preparing for these types of test items.

SOURCE: This material was adapted from a test matrix analysis prepared by the Long Beach Unified Public Schools for the Grade 3 Reading-Language Arts Test.

in support for those parents unable to help their own children (because of lack of time, skills, or English language skills, among other things). Promoting discussion among parents is a nearly surefire way of raising consciousness about what can be done to help students do their best.

We recommend that you do not put pressure on the parents to take tests or work with their children on the tests. The purpose in sending items to parents is to introduce the parents to the tests, so that they know what is expected of their children. A parent who knows even a little about what the child will be doing is a much better support for the child than a parent who knows nothing about the test.

EQUIPPING PARENTS TO MAKE GOOD PARTICIPATION AND ACCOMMODATION DECISIONS

Making sure that the parents know about the test is the first step in equipping parents to make good decisions about district and state tests. Two decisions to which parents must contribute, according to the Individuals With Disabilities Education Improvement Act of 2004 (IDEA 2004), are (1) the decision about which test the student will take, and (2) the decision about the use of accommodations during testing. To be able to make these decisions wisely, it is critical that parents have good information about the implications of each of the decisions as well as what the options are.

The excerpt in Box 9.2 is from a report produced by the Federation for Families of Children with Disabilities. It provides a strong rationale for why it is important to have students with disabilities participate in district and state assessments.

In the past, the only decisions that parents of students with disabilities had to make about the test participation of their children was whether they were going to take the test or be exempted from it. Of course, the Individualized Education Program (IEP) teams made those decisions, and often parents weren't even provided enough information about the options to make informed decisions.

Since the Individuals With Disabilities Education Act of 1997 (IDEA 97) and now IDEA 2004, however, parents are supposed to be partners in making decisions about how students participate, whether they take the same assessment as most other students in the state or they take an alternate assessment designed for those students unable to participate in the regular assessment even if provided with accommodations to give them access to that assessment.

Parents need to be given enough information to make good decisions about the assessment in which their children will participate, be it the regular assessment or alternate assessment. The key kinds of questions that they need to be made aware of and that you need to help them answer are as follows:

• *What is the purpose of the regular assessment?* It is especially important for parents to understand that there are specific reasons for their children to participate in assessments whether the purpose is for system accountability or student accountability. The reasons just differ.

Box 9.2

Excerpt From Federation of Families Report

Benefits to Students

Statewide assessments have enormous ramifications for students with disabilities. Benefits to students include

- **A Key to High Expectations:** The overall goal of our nation's many education reform initiatives is to raise the level of learning for all students, including students with disabilities. The goal is grounded in the belief that all students are capable of meeting much higher standards than have been expected of them in the past. Historically, expectations for students with disabilities have been appallingly low, as these students have been discouraged from participation in general curriculum studies. Students with disabilities must participate in assessments to ensure meaningful access to the same high curriculum and standards that drive education for all students.
- **School Accountability for All:** Participation in assessments sends the message that schools are accountable for all students reaching higher levels of learning. The higher expectations placed on schools can result in increased usage of accommodations or adaptations and other strategies to help students with disabilities reach higher standards.
- **A Role in Shaping Policies and Programs:** To help students meet higher standards, state and local education agencies are developing new instructional methods and technologies. Data from assessments can be used to gather information about promising practices and to improve programs. If students with disabilities are included in assessments, their needs will be considered in shaping education policies, programs, and practices.
- **High Stakes for Individual Students:** For individual students, the importance of assessments may be even more direct and critical. Increasingly, assessments are used as the basis for awarding diplomas or for gaining access to postsecondary opportunities. Students with disabilities must have equal opportunities to demonstrate their competencies in order to have full and equal access to future opportunities.

SOURCE: Reprinted with permission from Landau, J. K., Vohs, J. R., & Romano, C. A. (1998). *All kids count: Including students with disabilities in statewide assessment programs* (pp. 1-2). Boston, MA: Federation for Children with Special Needs, Parents Engaged in Educational Reform.

For system accountability, their participation helps to ensure that the system is held accountable for their performance. If schools or districts are not meeting the needs of all students, then this needs to be evident. Students with disabilities have the right to perform well, just like all other students; therefore, their performance also needs to be made evident.

For student accountability, one reason to have students participate is to ensure them access to diplomas. In many states (but not all), having the student not take a graduation exam may mean that the student will not receive the same kind of diploma as other students. In other states, these tests are used to make retention or grade-level promotion decisions.

• *What are the characteristics of students who should be taking an alternate assessment?* States and districts are required by the No Child Left Behind (NCLB) Act and IDEA 2004 to have guidelines for making decisions about who participates in alternate assessments. These guidelines should make it fairly evident to decision makers what the characteristics are of students taking each kind of assessment. Parents need to be familiar with these guidelines and how the characteristics defined in them (or implied by them) correspond to their own child's characteristics.

• *What kind of accommodations does my child need to be successful in school and in other situations? Can these be provided during assessments and still produce scores that have meaning?* Parents need to be aware that they have insights about their child that no one else may have. They may see the child providing himself or herself with accommodations during home life or during homework situations. Parents may provide accommodations to their child in the home that would be useful in the school environment as well. It is important for parents to understand what accommodations are and their purposes. Parents should also provide input to school personnel about what they know about accommodations needed and those used from the parent's perspective.

In addition, discussions need to occur about the "meaning" of scores from tests on which students have used certain accommodations. In every state, there are accommodations policies or guidelines that indicate whether a testing change is considered to produce a score that is not comparable to scores taken without the accommodation—some states label these testing changes as modifications or nonstandard administrations. Parents must be made aware of the terminology that is used in their state and district, of the specific nature of the testing changes recommended for their child, and of the consequences of using those accommodations (or modifications, or nonstandard administrations). Informed parents on this issue are strong resources. Uninformed parents are potential time bombs—ticking toward potential lawsuits.

• *What will the impact of participating in testing (either regular assessments or alternate assessments) be on my child? Will it be harmful to his or her motivation to learn or self-esteem?* Parents naturally have concerns about the potential impact of testing on their child. This is true whether or not the child has a disability, but the concern seems to be elevated for students with disabilities because many start with low expectations for them. The effect of this is compounded by the fact that low expectations often have resulted in instruction that has not pushed the student forward enough, with the inevitable result being continued low performance.

Adding to the negative impact attributed to testing is the fact that teachers, parents, and administrators do not (perhaps because they do not know how) provide the information and support to students before they sit down for an exam. Students need to be told the purpose of testing, just like teachers and parents are told. Students also need to be given details of what the testing is like, how long it lasts, where it is given, and a variety of other characteristics. They need to be provided with practice so that they are comfortable with the testing situation and procedures. In addition, they need to be informed about accommodations that are available to them, the importance of their performance, and other relevant characteristics that may apply to their specific locations.

All school personnel have a responsibility to ensure that students do their best, that they recognize the importance of the test, and that they are not made to feel that their participation is a negative thing for anyone. Parents should be supported and never be pressured to keep their children at home on the day of district or state testing.

HELPING PARENTS UNDERSTAND TEST RESULTS

In the past many district and state educational assessments were notorious for the incomprehensible information that they provided to parents. This should no longer be the case because most (but not all) district and state tests now use common words (such as *below basic*, *basic*, and *proficient*) to define student achievement or performance levels. However, we should realize that the use of common words does not necessarily make the meaning comprehensible. There is a great need for better communication about test results. No matter what the testing company may do to try to make the results of state and district assessments more comprehensible, it is educators who are ultimately responsible for ensuring that parents understand test results.

Several things need to be communicated to parents to ensure that they understand the results of testing. It is important for parents to be informed about the meaning of test results in general and the meaning of test results specifically for their child. Each of these is addressed here.

Understanding General Test Results

Because almost every district and state has its own testing program, it will be important for you to flesh out the information that we provide here and make it specific to your own testing environment. This should take only a little bit of time to do and will be well worth the effort. However, districts and states should be able to request that their testing programs provide the kinds of information that we present here. Generally, this will happen only if it is required in the contract set up with the test's developer.

Parents need to be provided with four essential pieces of information to have a basic understanding of overall test results: (1) the purpose of the test, (2) the content of the test, (3) the format of the test, and (4) how the test was administered. To this must then be added information on what is expected: How should students be performing? Several questions and answers for parents on these topics are provided in Box 9.3.

Box 9.3

Parent Questions and Answers About State and District Assessments

Question: Why do I need to know whether my state or district assessment is a norm-referenced assessment?

Answer: Norm-referenced tests (NRTs) are developed to enable a student to be compared to other students, or for a group of students (say, those in a school) to be compared to a group of students nationwide. This feature enables schools, districts, and states to know how they are performing in comparison to other schools, districts, or states. Although this seems to be important, NRTs have several limitations, one of which is that they do not directly assess standards; they assess a broad set of objectives that are not directly related to any one student's curriculum. In addition, they have other limitations for students with disabilities. One of these is that most NRTs allow relatively few accommodations to be used.

Question: Why is it important for my child to be included in assessments if their purpose is just to decide whether the school gets a reward for student performance? One student won't make a difference.

Answer: It is important that the school knows that every child counts. Although it is true that the score of one student may not make a big difference in the overall rating a school gets, it is very easy for one student to multiply into many students, and these students generally are those expected to perform less well on the assessment. Once students are not included in the assessment, there is not the urgency to worry about whether they are mastering the skills that will be on the test. And if there is no urgency to worry about them, then it is easy to forget about them. Furthermore, when decisions are based on data, the missing data from students who didn't take the test will have no influence on the reforms that are generated as a result of student performance. All of these together produce a situation in which students not only are excluded from the assessment, but also from the indirect benefits of reform and often also from the direct benefits of instruction.

Question: How can I tell whether the test my child is taking is based on standards, basic skills, or something else?

Answer: The best way to determine what is being measured is to ask. Often this information is provided in information about the test, but not always.

Question: My student has a learning disability. What kinds of test items are going to be easiest for my child, and what kinds of test items do I need to have him work on at home?

Answer: There is no simple answer to this question. The research does not give easy answers. Most likely, the "easiness of items" is going to be related to things other than simply whether they are multiple choice, essay, or performance events. Because of this, it is important that your child's teacher knows exactly what kinds of items are included in the test and that practice on these items is provided. The item types should not drive instruction, however. There is some research evidence that preparing the student to answer essay questions will also better prepare the student to answer multiple-choice questions.

Question: How can I help the IEP team make good decisions about the accommodations that my child will need during the state or district assessment?

Answer: Making decisions about accommodations should be a collaborative effort. You should provide information that supports the information that your child's teacher and other educators bring to the IEP team meeting. It is best to keep your input to what you know. Based on your knowledge of your child's learning experiences, you have a lot to say. Think about what helps your child get things done at home. Does he or she need to be in a distraction-free environment to finish tasks? Does he or she need frequent breaks to do a good job on household chores? Think about recreational activities, household chores, and skill learning, and bring information about these things to the IEP meeting.

The *purpose* of the test needs to be addressed in terms of two aspects: (1) whether the test will compare students to a standardization group or assess whether they have met a standard, and (2) whether there will be consequences for the school system (or aspects of it, such as teachers), for the student, or both. The first topic focuses on norm-referenced testing (NRT) and criterion-referenced testing (CRT); the second topic focuses on accountability.

Parents should be helped to understand the basic distinctions between NRTs and CRTs. Ways in which these differences can be explained are included in Box 9.4. A primary reason for making sure that parents have an understanding of the differences among test types is that whether a test is an NRT or a CRT often affects accommodation policies.

The consequences of the test need to be clear, defining what specifically will happen if students perform or do not perform in a specific way. Consequences for the school or district are defined for Title I schools by NCLB, and if this accountability system is in place in the student's school, it needs to be clearly explained. There are many materials provided by the U.S. Department of Education directly for parents and families that can help do this. The consequences are complicated, but graduated in scope, moving from the provision of choice options to the student to the eventual planning for restructuring of the school. Parents also need to know about any other types of accountability systems that might be in place that may put pressure on the schools or school staff. For example, some schools have decided to implement pay bonuses to teachers based on the performance of the students in their classes.

Parents and families also must be kept informed about consequences that exist for students. The most prominent student consequences are that a student might not receive a standard high school diploma if he or she does not earn a certain score on the graduation test. Or a student may not be promoted from one grade to another without earning a certain score. There are also consequences that involve a student not receiving credit for a course if a certain percentage of correct answers is not achieved, as in end-of-course exams. It is important to be very specific with parents, families, and guardians about the purpose and consequences of each and every test.

The notion that the purpose of district and state tests is to push the system to improve instruction probably will make little sense to the parent (and to others as well). Improving instruction directly for individual students is rarely

Box 9.4

Norm-Referenced Versus Criterion-Referenced Tests and Standards-Based Assessments

Norm-Referenced Tests: These tests are developed to measure a student's performance in comparison to the performance of other students. These tests are developed to create a spread of scores, so some students will score poorly and others will score well. A national sample of students takes the test, and the scores of students are compared to the scores of this national sample. Because the goal is to have all students take the test under the same conditions, relatively few accommodations are allowed.

Criterion-Referenced Tests: These tests are developed to measure a student's knowledge and skills, which are held up to a level of acceptable performance to indicate whether the student has reached the desired criterion. These tests also measure the student against a criterion, not against other students. Because having all students take the test under exactly the same conditions is not a goal of criterion-referenced tests, many more accommodations are allowed in criterion-referenced testing.

Standards-Based Assessment: These are tests (or other measures) that are criterion referenced, where the criterion is composed of standards identified by the state or district. Thus, the measurement is directly tied to instruction, if instruction is directly aligned to the standards. Like criterion-referenced tests, many accommodations are allowed during these assessments.

a result of state or district assessments. Rather, the improvement of instructional programs is a more realistic effect of these assessments. This in turn may have a direct effect on the instruction provided to individual students.

The *content* of the test also must be clearly defined for parents. Here we mean more than just the subject matter covered (such as reading, math, and writing). We also mean the nature of that content. For example, what is being measured—high standards or basic standards? Or is the content based on what students nationally are learning (such as in NRTs that use a pool of items that can be taken by students in any state)? Is the content directly related to what students are learning in class, or is it pushing the limits of what they are taught? Does the content reflect the minimum that students should know?

The *format* of the test may be a traditional multiple-choice test, a multiple-choice-plus-short-answer and/or extended-response test, a performance event, or a portfolio. The names of these formats should be translated for parents so that they are hearing both the current terminology and the terms with which they may be more familiar. Box 9.5 provides a quick guide for translating terminology for parents.

Information on *how the test is to be administered* is also important for parents to understand, so that they will know the conditions under which their child will take the test. The first step is to describe the requirements of the testing

Box 9.5

Guide for Translating Testing Terminology for Parents

Testing Term	Alternate Term	Explanation
Aggregate	Combine	The aggregation of test scores is the process of putting the scores from many students together to form a total picture. It is simply a process of combining scores, albeit sometimes in very complex ways.
Alternate assessment	Different assessment	Alternate assessments are mandated by federal law for those students who are unable to participate in the general assessment. The alternate assessment is simply a different assessment. It may or may not resemble the general assessment that it is an alternate to. In many states, the alternate assessment is a portfolio, while the general assessment is a paper-and-pencil test.
Disaggregate	Separate	The disaggregation of test scores is the process of separating out the scores of a group of students. Federal law requires that the scores of students with disabilities be disaggregated from the scores of other students and be aggregated with them.
Large-scale assessment	State or district test	Large-scale assessment simply means that the test was developed to be administered to large numbers of students, usually in groups. District and state tests are large-scale assessments.
Reliability	Consistency	Reliability is a psychometric term used to indicate the extent to which a score is (in very general terms) stable over time, the same if scored by two individuals, or the same if broken into two parts.
Rubric	Rules	Rubrics are descriptions of a test performance that support scoring guides, which are used to indicate the closeness of a student to a standard. The rubrics define what kind of a performance is below basic and what is considered proficient.
Validity	Accuracy	Validity is the accuracy of a measure derived from a test. It indicates that the test measures what the test developer wanted it to measure.

situation. The second step is a discussion of the accommodations that may be used during the assessment.

The *requirements* of the testing situation include whether the test is timed, whether it involves group work or individualized responding, whether it is completed over time (e.g., three days during a week) or on one specific day, and whether it is administered in the regular classroom or somewhere else. It also includes whether the test is a paper-and-pencil test or is provided through other media (e.g., computers). All of these kinds of requirements are important to include because they set the stage for understanding the accommodations that may be used during the assessment.

Understanding the *accommodations* is another important part of preparing parents to understand the test results. It is critical for parents (and students, as they mature) to be aware of accommodation needs. It is also important for them to understand how these needs relate to what the test allows and what will happen if the student uses accommodations that the test does not allow.

Many excellent brochures have been developed by states to explain accommodation policies to parents. Many of these can be viewed on state Web sites. What is much less clear (and rarely explained to anyone) is what happens when a student needs something other than what is allowed.

Most district and state tests do not allow the reading test to be read to the student. Why? Because, it is argued, reading the test to the student confounds the construct being assessed, namely, reading ability. But what if a student truly cannot read but can understand text that is read to him or her? Some would argue that if you allowed this, you would really be testing listening comprehension, and therefore the student must be excluded because the test would no longer be evaluating reading skills. Thus, parents and schools end up with no information on the child. In our opinion, it is better to have the student participate in the assessment, using the accommodations that the child needs, and then disaggregate the data of that student (as well as other students using "nonallowed" accommodations) so that there is some evidence about their performance. This is better than having no data at all.

Another approach, now embraced in only a few locations, would argue that for a student who truly is dyslexic it is important to assess how proficient the student is at obtaining information from written text. How this information is taken in by the student is not as important as determining whether it is. Thus, in this example, allowing the reading test to be read to the student is okay, meaning that the student can use this accommodation, and the scores are reported. More recent considerations are the topics of current research. For example, is it possible to read certain portions of the test, but not other portions, and still have a meaningful score (similar to tests that allow a calculator to be used on certain portions but not other portions)? Or, is it possible to score the test in ways that separate out those items that are decoding items from others for students who must have the entire test read to them. Stay tuned for much activity in the area of nonallowed accommodations, especially those that involve reading. It is especially important to keep parents aware of these advances as well.

Parents also need to be helped to engage in more long-range thinking about accommodations and their child. For example, they need to realize that the need for accommodations can change over time. This can happen as the child gains skills that take over for previously needed accommodations. Nearly all students also go through a period during which they do not want to use any accommodations; they don't want to be set apart from their peers by their need for accommodations. Recognizing this ahead of time can help parents talk to their child about this: that is, about the consequences of not using an accommodation that is needed, about talking to their peers about their accommodations, and so on.

Parents should also be aware of the need to assist their child in recognizing accommodation needs and in advocating for their own accommodations. As children get older, there is a tendency for teachers and others to rely more on what the student says than on what may be on a piece of paper. When the child enters middle school or high school, teachers often have less access to IEPs and other documents that describe the student's accommodation needs. Thus, the student must be aware of his or her own needs and must know how to ask for accommodations to meet those needs. This is an essential skill that should be a part of every transition program.

Understanding Their Child's Test Results

Not long ago, we were listening to a group of parents talk about their children's scores on the tests that their school districts administered every spring. One parent mentioned that her son had received three scores in reading and three in math. None of them made any sense. He remembered that they were all percentages, but the reading ones were 25%, 55%, and 40%. He remembered that there were three more scores for math. One score was the same, 55%, but the others were completely different (90% and 75%). No one had explained the tests or their scores to the parent.

It turned out that the district used a nationally and locally normed reading test and a criterion-referenced mathematics test. The score that the parent was seeing in reading reflected three elements: (1) how the student did compared to other students in the same grade in the district, (2) how the student performed compared to other students in the same grade in the nation, and (3) the percentage of items attempted that were correct. The math scores, however, reflected (1) the percentage of items correct, (2) the percentage of items attempted, and (3) the percentage of students obtaining the same score or lower. This example demonstrates why it is important for parents to know about the tests and to be provided with clear-cut, easy-to-remember scores.

Another example is very different. This parent could only remember that she saw a lot of letters on the test (such as SS or M) and that they were defined in footnotes. But the footnote just contained words like "scale score" and "mean" without telling what those words meant. The results, according to the parent, were meaningless.

Even parents who get test results that come back with words like "basic," "proficient," and "beginner" do not understand what they really mean unless they are defined. In addition, parents should be given examples of what those scores mean in actual performance.

Several excellent Web sites and booklets for parents provide this type of information in clear and concise ways. Even though these materials are useful, we think that it is important to apply that clarity to the actual scores that parents see. This must be done either by the test development company, the state department, or the district or school itself.

What kinds of information do we think parents need? In addition to the student's scores (with explanations and examples attached), they need to know the content of the test, the nature of the items, and whether the district's scores reflect performances on basic standards, high standards, or some other entity (such as CRTs or NRTs). They also need to know the consequences of the test and any challenges that existed during the testing or scoring (such as accommodations that the student was not able to use or that produced a score that could not be aggregated).

Working with the test developer to produce appropriate materials is probably the best and most efficient approach to meeting the need for parent information. Most often this collaboration takes place at the state level between the assessment office and the test contractor. However, at the district level much information and materials can be produced that are parent friendly. Putting it on the Web is good but does not yet meet the needs of all parents. Thus, if neither of these exist, it is critical to get together with parents to define what kind of information they need and then either hire a contractor to develop the materials or do it yourself. There should never be an excuse for not providing parents with enough information about testing programs, tests, scores, and their consequences. Box 9.6 contains more information on parent centers and other resources.

States and districts often develop reports that portray in one way or another the scores that students earn on tests. Recently, there has been an increased

---

Box 9.6

Resource Centers and Materials for Parents

Several parent centers now produce information directly relevant to district and state tests. In the past, these centers generally knew only about testing for eligibility determination or for reevaluation purposes. Here are some centers that are worth connecting with:

Parent Information and Resource Centers (PIRCs), one-stop resource centers funded by the U.S. Department of Education to provide training, information, and technical assistance within states. Eighty exist across the contiguous U.S., Alaska, Hawaii, Pacific Rim Islands, Puerto Rico, and the Virgin Islands. See www.pirc-info.net/index.asp to find the PIRC in your area.

Parent Training and Information Centers (PTIs) in each state help parents participate more effectively with professionals to meet the educational needs of their children with disabilities. See www.taalliance.org/centers/index.htm to find the PTI in your area.

The ALLIANCE, Technical Assistance ALLIANCE for Parent Centers, a federally supported project within the Parent Advocacy Coalition for Educational Rights (PACER) Center to provide national technical assistance to parent centers (8161 Normandale Blvd., Minneapolis, MN 55437; Voice 888-248-0822 or 952-838-9000; TTY 952-838-0190; Fax: 952-838-0199; www.taalliance.org)

Box 9.7

Example of Information Presented in State Report

Putting Scores in Context: Looking at the Big Picture

As we step back and look at the results from these tests, there are several important points to remember:

- **These are HIGH standards.** For example, reading means not only being able to understand words but being able to analyze and interpret texts. For students to truly achieve fluency in math, they must be able to complete a math computation *and* apply mathematical concepts to create equations, solve problems, and explain how results are derived.
- **The WASL** [Washington Assessment of Student Learning] **is *just one measure* of student achievement.** Teacher grades, classroom assignments, student projects, and scores on other standardized tests should all be used to get a broader sense of student achievement.
- **Washington's assessment system is flexible.** While all students must be assessed in terms of their learning, . . . the [state assessment], in its present form, may not be adequate to assess all students. [The state education department] has already developed alternate assessment guidelines for students in special education and is also developing new ways to address the needs of English-language learners.
- **The high academic standards measured by the WASL reflect the challenges students will face in our complex world.** Students who don't meet the standards should be encouraged to continue working hard to gain these skills and not feel discouraged by their score on a single test.
- **Only by looking at the data over time will we begin to see patterns emerge.** In the meantime, we can be confident that steady progress will be made as we sharpen out focus on essential academic learning requirements.

SOURCE: Reprinted from *Reaching higher: A parent's guide to the Washington assessment of student learning* (prepared by the Office of Superintendent of Public Instruction) (p. 7), Revised June 2003.

interest in reporting so that parents can understand what test results mean. Box 9.7 contains an excerpt from a report for parents in Washington state. It would serve educators well to provide these kinds of explanations for parents or, if they do not exist, to develop them.

SUMMARY

In this chapter, we highlighted several things that parents and guardians need to know and that you as an educator are responsible for helping the parent to learn. In this chapter is information about testing in general and the tests administered by the state or district in particular.

This chapter probably has given you lots of ideas about what parents need. You may be questioning whether it is really your responsibility to provide this to parents. We answer this question with an unqualified *yes*, if not for the parents themselves, but for student benefit. Informed parents can better support what schools expect of all students during testing. Parents who do not understand the test that is being given to their children are more likely to question the results and the test itself. They are more likely to cast blame for low scores than are those parents who really understand the assessment and who have worked to assist their child in preparing for the test. And, as we all know, angry parents often turn to lawyers to relieve their feelings of frustration and explore their options. Communication is Key.

TEST YOUR KNOWLEDGE

Complete the following fill-in-the-blank statements. Reread parts of this chapter if the words that go in the blanks are not obvious to you.

1. _____ need to know about the purpose of the test, the content areas tested, the types of items that are included in the test, how long the test or each part of the test usually takes, where and how the test is usually administered, and the consequences of the child's performance on the test.

2. A test _____ can be simplified or rearranged to help parents better understand skill and item emphasis of the assessment.

3. A strategy that is usually helpful to parents is to give them a sample _____.

4. Making sure that the parent knows about the test is the first step in equipping parents to make good _____ about district and state tests.

5. Parents are partners in making decisions about *how* students _____ in district and state tests.

6. In the past, district and state educational assessments were notorious for the _____ information that they provided to parents.

7. Districts and states should be able to request that their testing programs provide good _____ for parents.

8. There are excellent examples of _____ that states have developed to explain accommodation policies to parents.

9. Even parents who get test results with words like "basic" and "proficient" may not understand what they really mean unless they are _____.

10. Working with the _____ _____ is probably the most efficient approach to meeting the need for parent information.

ANSWERS

1. Parents (p. 166)

2. matrix (p. 166)

3. test (p. 166)

4. decisions (p. 168)

5. participate (p. 168)

6. incomprehensible (p. 171)

7. information (p. 171)

8. brochures (p. 176)

9. defined (p. 177)

10. test developer/company (p. 178)

REFLECTIONS ON CHANGE

See Appendix A for the Reflections on Change activity for this chapter (p. 193).

RECOMMENDED RESOURCES

Bigge, J. L., & Stump, C. S. (1999). *Curriculum, assessment, and instruction for students with disabilities.* Belmont, CA: Wadsworth.

Cookson, P., Halberstam, J., Berger, K., & Mescavage, S. (1998). *A parent's guide to standardized tests in school.* Norwalk, CT: Learning Express.

Goldberg, M., Guy, B., & Moses, J. A. (1999). *Education reform: What does it mean for students with disabilities?* (NTN Parent Brief). Minneapolis: University of Minnesota, National Transition Network.

Landau, J. K., Vohs, J. R., & Romano, C. A. (1998). *All kids count: Including students with disabilities in statewide assessment programs* (PEER Project). Boston, MA: Federation for Children with Special Needs.

PBS Frontline. (2002). *Our schools: A guide for parents.* Retrieved September 12, 2004, from www.pbs.org/wgbh/pages/frontline/shows/schools/etc/guide.html

Thurlow, M. L., Elliott, J. L., & Ysseldyke, J. E. (2003). *Testing students with disabilities: Practical strategies for complying with district and state requirements (2nd ed.).* Thousand Oaks, CA: Corwin.

U.S. Department of Education. (2003). *No Child Left Behind: A parents guide.* Available at www.ed.gov/nclb

INTERNET RESOURCES

Parent Alliance: www.pacer.org/index.html

7-9 Self-Check: Where Do I Stand?

Evaluate and reflect on the following statements as a personal survey of where you stand in relation to the information presented. Base your assessment on the topics that are presented in this book and what you think you already know and are doing.

Self-Check for Chapter 7

- I recognize the dual system of educating general and special education students that has developed over the years. However, I believe that good teaching is good teaching, and effective instructional strategies work for all kids in general education and special education.
- Teaching is hard work; that's for sure! However, I recognize that expectations for students with disabilities are not always the same as for general education students. I am making sure that the curriculum and materials I use in the classroom or with individual students in the general setting parallel as much as possible the standards worked on by all students.
- I see how the focus on assessments and high test scores has affected instruction in the classroom. Teachers are stressed out about how their students will do on the tests. I know what I need to do to improve the performance of my students: Teach!
- I realize that education, in general, has not done a good job in evaluating the effectiveness of instruction. When students perform poorly on classroom and/or district assessments, too often the students are blamed. I now know better! I work every day to have instruction make a difference in students' lives rather than a predictor about their lives.

Self-Check for Chapter 8

- I recognize that alternate assessments are changing as we better understand the nature of learning and our expectations for academic learning for students with the most significant cognitive disabilities.

- I understand that instruction for students with significant cognitive disabilities should be aligned to grade-level content standards, but that this does not mean that other important skills, such as functional skills, should be forgotten.
- I realize that because so much of our knowledge about alternate assessments and the students who participate in them is changing. I will need to continue to pay attention to what is happening in this area and watch frequently for new information.

Self-Check for Chapter 9

- I realize that parents, guardians, and other family members are an important part of improving the test performance of students with disabilities. I have a plan for engaging parents in the testing process, from encouraging participation in decisions at the IEP meeting, to providing awareness materials about the nature of the test, to helping them understand the results of testing.
- I know how to explain the test, the testing terms, and the results to parents and have a set of materials to also convey this information.
- I encourage parents to help their children prepare for tests in whatever way they can, realizing that this may vary widely among the parents and guardians of students for whom I am responsible. I respect this variation and create innovative strategies for students whose parents cannot be as involved as other parents.

Appendix A

Reflections on Change

An innovation is only as good as one's understanding of it. In any field, especially education, there is a critical need for process, training, and professional development for those who work in what we call the trenches—in other words, those who face students on a daily basis with the huge responsibility of educating them (and, of course, improving performance on assessments). The relatively recent changes in federal laws have created the impetus for the development of inclusive accountability and assessment systems, which, as you know, has not been universally accepted with open arms by all. In fact, some of the strongest resistance often comes from educators in special education.

OVERVIEW

Best practice for instruction means assessing the level and understanding where the students are currently, for new or revisited information. This goes for adult students as well! With any new topic, there is a continuum of knowledge that ranges from awareness to synthesis and application. Using the Concerns-Based Adoption Model (CBAM) by Hall, Wallace, and Dossett (1973), you can get a "heartbeat" on where folks are, which can help drive the planning and delivery of quality professional development or develop an action plan for change.

The basic premise of CBAM is that adults differ in their ability and readiness to accept changes and innovations. We provide you both with an overview of the CBAM model and suggestions for ways to use it in your efforts to train personnel in areas that are focused on improving the performance of students with disabilities. The following are the CBAM stages and our adaptation to tailor it to our topic:

Awareness—This stage is characterized as very low adult involvement. Adults either don't know or act as if they don't know much about instruction, accountability, and assessment as it relates to all students, particularly for students with disabilities.

Informational—This stage is characterized by general awareness and interest, but still relatively little involvement. Here you may find people who acknowledge that something is going on related to students with disabilities and assessment, but they believe it will not impact them.

Personal—In this stage the "aha" phenomenon begins. People begin to see and consider the impact of the innovations, policies, and practices on themselves. For example, site administrators may begin to be concerned as to whether students with disabilities will "count" in their building test scores; teachers may begin to count the number of students in their general education classes and those that require accommodations in instruction and on classroom assessments. The reality of participation of students with disabilities in state and district assessment begins to set in.

Management—This stage is characterized by informed personnel who now realize that the changes in federal requirements for students with disabilities are here to stay. They begin to focus on methodologies and strategies to improve the performance of students with disabilities, both in instruction and assessment. There is elevated need to find out what to do and how to do it.

Consequence—In this stage, people zero in on outcomes of instruction and assessment. They begin to raise questions about resources, including the opportunity for students to learn what is expected, fairness of existing practices, and ways that can accelerate improved results for student learning.

Collaboration— This is a learning-in-process stage. Personnel collaborate with others, especially those with knowledge and experience in working with students with disabilities, with the goal of learning more about these students and their needs and capabilities. They *get it*. They see the connection between effective standards-based instruction and improved performance for all students, including students with disabilities.

Refocusing—This stage is characterized by interest and efforts surrounding the refinement of implemented strategies, plans, and methodologies. There is a fresh, focused effort in the development and improvement of results-based instruction for all students.

We have taken the CBAM and made suggestions about how it can be tailored to proactively manage each stage you will, no doubt, encounter along the way. Each stage is highlighted with some general activities that can be provided to help you move through the model.

Stage	*Activity*
Awareness	Dissemination of articles or position papers published by recognized organizations
	Faculty meetings, workshops, and overviews
	Ongoing staff meetings
	Posting of belief statements or signs reflecting the way of the imminent future
Informational	Reading lists, video series, satellite conferences on related topics
	Presentations from within-district personnel who have innovative practices in place
	Testimonials of "where we've been and where we are now" from within or outside your school district
	Visits with other schools or school districts' programs
	Newsletters and other easy-reading professional literature on teaching strategies, accommodation, assessment, and accountability
	Full-day workshops or inservices developed from specific needs identified within the school or district
Personal	Tailored topical sessions that provide personnel with opportunities for discussion and reflection
	Testimonials of "where we've been and where we are now" from within or outside your school district
Communication Forums	Discussions with parents, students, and others impacted by current practices and the proposed improvements to them
	Case studies of turnaround schools and programs and the benefits to students
Management	Practical inservices and information on how-to's
	Group planning and problem-solving sessions
	Networking with other districts and states working to improve performance of students with disabilities on assessments
	Exploring national technical assistance and dissemination networks
	Applications for grants and foundation money
Consequence	Selected current educational articles/reviews on legal consequences for noninclusive and accommodation systems
	Legal briefs or stance from the Office for Civil Rights on opportunity to learn and assessment cases
	Mapping out strategies and outcomes that have set benchmark dates for efforts
	Forums to facilitate discussion about questions, concerns, and challenges in implementing effective instruction to improve student performance

Collaboration	Instructional/assessment "swat" teams to coach and monitor the integrity of program implementation
	Create CIA collaborative committees—curriculum, instruction, and assessment
	Time to collaborate on the inputs, processes, and outcomes
	Cross-departmental meetings
	Coteaching across content areas
Refocusing	National conferences
	Revisiting strategic plan and benchmarks
	Action research and evaluation on "how are we doing?"
	Talking to the students and parents—what insights do they offer?
	Planned activities for rejuvenation and recognition of progress
	Rewarding and reinforcing efforts to move to more comprehensive instructional programs for students

These are but a few brainstorming suggestions to use as a springboard for each stage of the model. You know your situation best. Tailor activities as appropriate to your current climate. Turn this model into a needs assessment by placing statements on a Lickert scale. The needs assessment can simply depict current issues and/or key elements to reform activities at hand. Have people rate each item from 1 to 7, where 1 is awareness and 7 is refocusing.

Example CBAM assessment

Item 1

1 2 3 4 5 6 7   I am aware of the recent changes in federal laws that make it necessary for us to review our instructional and assessment practices for all students, including students with disabilities.

Item 2

1 2 3 4 5 6 7   I have a complete understanding of the ways students with disabilities participate in assessments—standard assessment, assessment with accommodations, or alternate assessments.

Item 3

1 2 3 4 5 6 7   I know how to link student IEPs to the standards all students are working toward.

Item 4

1 2 3 4 5 6 7   I understand the purpose and use of accommodations.

Item 5

1 2 3 4 5 6 7   I have a clear understanding of how to make decisions about instructional and assessment accommodations for students.

For each chapter in this book (except Chapter 1), we have developed a corresponding CBAM inventory for you to use—with yourself or others—as you progress through the issues surrounding improving the test performance of students with disabilities. Use each CBAM as an inventory of five key concepts that are important to each chapter's topic. Feel free to adopt or change any and all of the CBAMs to meet the needs of what you are using them for.

Remember, the Reflection on Change CBAMs are meant to help you think about possible or needed change for policies and practices currently going on in your own backyard. We have selected five big ideas from each chapter that we think will be the most critical to inventory in your own situation.

Good luck and have fun!

Chapter 2   Standards-Based Assessment and Instruction

Item 1

1   2   3   4   5   6   7   I am aware of several basic principles that are needed to ensure standards-based reform and accountability have a solid foundation on which to build.

Item 2

1   2   3   4   5   6   7   I am aware of the importance of linking, and know how to link IEP goals to content standards.

Item 3

1   2   3   4   5   6   7   I understand and know how to take a content standard and unpack its concepts, vocabulary, and prerequisite skills.

Item 4

1   2   3   4   5   6   7   Once a content standard is unpacked, I know how to create a blueprint for instruction that will provide me both formative and summative assessments aligned with instruction.

Item 5

1   2   3   4   5   6   7   I understand the importance of leadership as a critical aspect to accountability and educational reform. Walkthroughs are one example of accountability-based leadership.

Chapter 3   Using Data to Drive Instruction

Item 1

1   2   3   4   5   6   7   I understand the importance and the reasons behind why there are federal laws that now mandate the inclusion of all students, including students with disabilities, in accountability and assessment systems.

Item 2

1 2 3 4 5 6 7 I understand the importance and the value behind disaggregating assessment and achievement data in a variety of ways (e.g., gender, ethnicity, type of disability, grade level).

Item 3

1 2 3 4 5 6 7 I know that grades are only one way, albeit an important way, to examine whether instruction and programs are having a positive impact on student learning.

Item 4

1 2 3 4 5 6 7 I know that there are multiple variables that impact student performance and that it is important to be able to tease them out (e.g., weak test-taking strategies, lack of prerequisite skills).

Item 5

1 2 3 4 5 6 7 I am aware that regardless of the laws, there are people who will look for loopholes around the accountability system rather than work toward ways to improve the achievement of all students, including students with disabilities.

Chapter 4 Making Sound Accommodations Decisions

Item 1

1 2 3 4 5 6 7 I recognize the complexities in accommodation research and know how to separate opinion from research findings.

Item 2

1 2 3 4 5 6 7 I have a clear understanding of the basic considerations in making good decisions about accommodations.

Item 3

1 2 3 4 5 6 7 I know the steps to take to identify accommodations for individual students.

Item 4

1 2 3 4 5 6 7 I know how to document accommodations on the IEP, and I know the requirements for updating accommodations on a timely basis for testing.

Item 5

1 2 3 4 5 6 7 I have applied information about nonstandard accommodations to my own state's policies, so I am confident of what to do in challenging situations, such as when a student needs an accommodation that may produce an automatic low score for the school.

Chapter 5   Preparing Students for Testing

Item 1

1   2   3   4   5   6   7   I am aware that test scores can improve significantly just from direct instruction in how to prepare for testing.

Item 2

1   2   3   4   5   6   7   I am aware of the general areas that are important to and underscore test preparation for the classroom, district, and/or state assessment.

Item 3

1   2   3   4   5   6   7   I am familiar with ways to incorporate good instruction and varied methods and formats to help prepare students, on a daily basis, for assessment.

Item 4

1   2   3   4   5   6   7   I am aware of the impact of needed accommodations on student test performance. I am also aware that it is incredibly important to communicate these student needs to all teachers. It is important to check for understanding when discussing accommodations with teachers.

Item 5

1   2   3   4   5   6   7   I am aware of the importance of students becoming their own advocates for their testing needs, especially as they get older.

Chapter 6   Addressing the Needs of IEP/ELLs

Item 1

1   2   3   4   5   6   7   I recognize the growing population of students who are English language learners (ELLs) with disabilities and the need to carefully plan for ways to improve their achievement on standards-based assessments.

Item 2

1   2   3   4   5   6   7   I know that while NCLB may not require the disaggregation of data on IEP/ELLs, there are many good reasons to do so.

Item 3

1   2   3   4   5   6   7   I understand the need for accommodations that are linguistic in nature as well as those that meet disability needs.

Item 4

1   2   3   4   5   6   7   I know the instructional approaches that researchers have identified as effective for IEP/ELLs.

Item 5

1   2   3   4   5   6   7   I know the instructional strategies that teachers perceive to be effective within a standards-based educational system for IEP/ELLs.

Chapter 7   Improving Performance on General Assessments Through Instruction

Item 1

1   2   3   4   5   6   7   The role of teachers is not only to teach but also to create an environment where students can learn.

Item 2

1   2   3   4   5   6   7   I understand that student failure is not always just student related. Rather, failure can also be a result of a poorly implemented instructional environment.

Item 3

1   2   3   4   5   6   7   I understand the concept that accountability should be reciprocal.

Item 4

1   2   3   4   5   6   7   The planning pyramid allows us to look at instruction in a way that helps prioritize within the context of students' abilities.

Item 5

1   2   3   4   5   6   7   I understand the conceptual model of planning, managing, delivering, and evaluating instruction as a key element to setting up the instructional environment of success.

Chapter 8   Improving the Performance on Alternate Assessment Through Instruction

Item 1

1   2   3   4   5   6   7   I completely understand that alternate assessments are still evolving yet can be implemented well as they are being improved.

Item 2

1   2   3   4   5   6   7   I recognize the most common approaches to alternate assessments—collections of evidence, performance assessments, and checklists—as well as variations of them.

Item 3

1   2   3   4   5   6   7   I understand that the content standards for the alternate assessment may be described in terms of its essence or may be expanded to apply to students with significant cognitive disabilities.

Item 4

1 2 3 4 5 6 7 I know the importance of holding high expectations for all students, particularly those students participating in the alternate assessment.

Item 5

1 2 3 4 5 6 7 I am aware of the transformation that it takes to provide standards-based, grade-level instruction to students with significant cognitive disabilities.

Chapter 9   Parent Support for Student Learning

Item 1

1 2 3 4 5 6 7 I recognize the importance of making sure parents know everything possible about assessments so they can support their children's performance.

Item 2

1 2 3 4 5 6 7 I know the key kinds of questions and answers that parents need to be made aware of to be able to make good decisions.

Item 3

1 2 3 4 5 6 7 I completely understand the critical importance of helping parents understand test results and how to help them in that understanding.

Item 4

1 2 3 4 5 6 7 I am aware of basic terms that I need to translate for parents so that I do not seem to use jargon with them.

Item 5

1 2 3 4 5 6 7 I want to have parents as my partners in improving the performance of students with disabilities in my school.

Appendix B

Technical Assistance and Dissemination Networks

For more information on research and development efforts in the areas of instruction, assessment, and accountability, contact the following organizations:

Institute of Education Sciences
U.S. Department of Education
555 New Jersey Avenue, NW
Washington, DC 20208-5500
Telephone: 1-800-USA-LEARN
TTY: 1-800-437-0833
Fax: 202-401-0689
Web: www.ed.gov/offices/IES

Office of Special Education and Rehabilitative Services
U.S. Department of Education
400 Maryland Avenue, SW
Washington, DC 20202-7100
Telephone: 202-245-7468
Web: www.ed.gov/offices/OSERS

National Center on Educational Outcomes
University of Minnesota
350 Elliott Hall
75 East River Road
Minneapolis, MN 55455
Telephone: 612-626-1530
Fax: 612-624-0879
Web: www.nceo.info

National Center for Research on Evaluation, Standards, and Student Testing
UCLA CSE/CRESST
300 Charles E. Young Drive North
GSE&IS Bldg. 3rd Floor
Los Angeles, CA 90095-1522
Telephone: 310-206-1532
Fax: 310-825-3883
Web: www.cresst96.cse.ucla.edu

For a state and local policy perspective, contact the following organizations:

National Association of State Boards of Education (NASBE)
277 South Washington Street, Suite 100
Alexandria, VA 22314
Telephone: 703-684-4000
Fax: 703-836-2313
Web: www.nasbe.org

Center for Policy Research in Education (CPRE)
2440 Market Street, Suite 560
Philadelphia, PA 19104-3325
Telephone: 215-573-0700
Fax: 215-573-7914
Web: www.cpre.org

National Association of State Directors of Special Education (NASDSE)
1800 Diagonal Road, Ste 320
King Street Station I
Alexandria, VA 22314
Telephone: 703-519-3800
TDD: 703-519-7008
Fax: 703-519-3808
Web: www.nasdse.org

For state-based regional resource centers, contact the following organizations:

Federal Resource Center for Special Education (FRC)
Academy for Educational Development
1825 Connecticut Avenue NW, Ste 900
Washington, DC 20009
Telephone: 202-884-8215; TTY: 202-884-8200
Fax: 202-884-8443
Web: www.dssc.org/frc
E-mail: frc@federalresourcecenter.org

Region 1: Northeast (Connecticut, Maine, Massachusetts, New Hampshire, New Jersey, New York, Rhode Island, Vermont)

> Northeast Regional Resource Center (NERRC)
> Learning Innovations at WestEd
> 20 Winter Sport Lane
> Williston, VT 05495
> Telephone: 802-951-8226
> TTY: 802-951-8213
> Fax: 802-951-8222
> Web: www.wested.org/nerrc/
> E-mail: nerrc@aol.com

Region 2: Mid-South (Delaware, District of Columbia, Kentucky, Maryland, North Carolina, South Carolina, Tennessee, Virginia, West Virginia)

> Alliance for Systems Change and Mid-South Regional Resource Center (MSRRC)
> Interdisciplinary Human Development Institute/UK
> 1 Quality Street, Suite 722
> Lexington, KY 40507
> Telephone: 859-257-4921
> TTY: 859-257-2903
> Fax: 859-257-4353
> Web: www.ihdi.uky.edu/msrrc

Region 3: Southeast Regional Resource Center (Alabama, Arkansas, Florida, Georgia, Louisiana, Mississippi, Oklahoma, Texas, Puerto Rico, U.S. Virgin Islands)

> Southeast Regional Resource Center (SERRC)
> Auburn University Montgomery
> PO Box 244023
> Montgomery, AL 36124
> Telephone: 334-244-3100
> Fax: 334-244-3101
> Web: http//edla.aum.edu/serrc/serrc/.html
> E-mail: bbeale@edla.aum.edu

Region 4: North Central Regional Resource Center (Illinois, Indiana, Iowa, Michigan, Minnesota, Missouri, Ohio, Pennsylvania, Wisconsin)

> North Central Regional Resource Center
> Institute on Community Integration
> University of Minnesota
> 12 Pattee Hall, 150 Pillsbury Drive SE
> Minneapolis, MN 55455
> Telephone: 612-624-9722
> Fax: 612-624-9344
> E-mail: ncrrc@umn.edu

Region 5: Mountain Plains Regional Resource Center (Arizona, Colorado, Kansas, Montana, Nebraska, New Mexico, North Dakota, South Dakota, Utah, Wyoming)

Mountain Plains Regional Resource Center (MPRRC)
Utah State University
1780 North Research Parkway, Ste 112
Logan, UT 84341
Telephone: 435-752-0238; TTY 435-753-9750
Fax: 435-753-9750
Web: www.usu.edu/mprrc
E-mail: cope@cc.usu.edu

Region 6: Western Regional Resource Center (Alaska, California, Hawaii, Idaho, Nevada, Oregon, Washington, American Samoa, the Federated States of Micronesia, the Commonwealth of the Northern Marianna Islands, Guam, the Republic of the Marshall Islands, the Republic of Palau)

Western Regional Resource Center (WRRC)
1268 University of Oregon
Eugene, OR 97403-1268
Telephone: 541-346-5641; TTY: 541-346-0367
Fax: 541-346-0322
Web: http://interact.uoregon.edu/wrrc/wrrc.html
E-mail: wrrc@oregon.uoregon.edu

Other Technical Assistance and Dissemination Networks

National Dissemination Center for Children with Disabilities (NICHCY)
PO Box 1492
Washington, DC 20031-1492
Telephone: 202-884-8200; TTY 800-695-0285
Fax: 202-884-8441
Web: www.nichcy.org
E-mail: nichcy@aed.org

Council for Exceptional Children
1110 Glebe Road, Suite 300
Arlington, VA 22091-1589
Telephone: 703-620-3660, 800-CEC-SPED
Fax: 703-264-9494
Web: www.cec.sped.org/

Parents

Technical Assistance ALLIANCE for Parent Centers
PACER Center
8161 Normandale Blvd.

Minneapolis, MN 55437-1044
Telephone: 952-838-9000; Toll free 888-248-0822
TTY: 952-838-0190
Fax: 952-838-0199
Web: www.taalliance.org
E-mail: alliance@taalliance.org

Early Childhood

National Early Childhood Technical Assistance System (NECTAS)
Campus Box 8040
UNC-CH
Chapel Hill, NC 27599-8040
Telephone: 919-962-2001; TTY 919-843-3269
Fax: 919-966-7463
Web: www.nectac.org
E-mail: nectac@unc.edu

Other

Council of Chief State School Officers
One Massachusetts Avenue, NW
Suite 700
Washington, DC 20001-1431
Telephone: 202-336-7000
Fax: 202-408-8072
Web: www.ccsso.org

Education Commission of the States
700 Broadway, #1200
Denver, CO 80203-3460
Telephone: 303-299-3600
Fax: 303-296-8332
Web: www.ecs.org

Education Resources Information Center (ERIC)
ERIC Project
c/o Computer Sciences Corporation
4483-A Forbes Blvd.
Lanham, MD 20706
Telephone: 1-800-LET-ERIC (800-538-3742)
Web: www.eric.ed.gov

Education Trust
1250 H Street NW, Suite 700
Washington, DC 20005
Telephone: 202-293-1217
Fax: 202-293-2605
Web: www.edtrust.org

U.S. Department of Education
400 Maryland Avenue, SW
Washington, DC 20202
Telephone: 800-USA-LEARN
Web: www.ed.gov

What Works Clearinghouse
2277 Research Boulevard, MS 6M
Rockville, MD 20850
Telephone: 1-866-WWC-9799
Fax: 301-519-6760
E-mail: info@whatworks.ed.gov

Here are some additional Web sites not listed in the chapters:

Education Newsletters:

This site connects to more than 135 education newsletters within a directory of more than 5,000: www.newsletteraccess.com/

Federal and State Education Organizations: Links to national and state education organizations: http://wdcrobcolpol.ed.gov/Programs/EROD/

Individuals with Disabilities Education Improvement Act of 2004 (IDEA 2004): Here you will find the law for the act: www.ed.gov/policy/

No Child Left Behind of 2001 (NCLB): Here you will find the law for the act: www.ed.gov/policy/elsec/leg/esea02/index.html

National Clearinghouse for English Language Acquisition: NCELA collects, analyzes, synthesizes, and disseminates information about language instruction educational programs for ELLs: www.ncela.gwu.edu

THOMAS: Legislative Information on the Internet: You will find Congress floor activities of the week, the status of major legislation, committee reports, and more: http://thomas.loc.gov/

References

Algozzine, B., Ysseldyke, J., & Elliott, V. (1997). *Strategies and tactics for effective instruction* (2nd ed.). Longmont, CO: Sopris West.

Browder, D. (2001). *Curriculum and assessment for students with moderate and severe disabilities.* New York: Guilford.

Elliott, J., Algozzine, B., & Ysseldyke, J. (1998). *Timesavers for educators.* Longmont, CO: Sopris West.

Gall, M. D., Gall, J. P., Jacobsen, D. R., & Bullock, T. L. (1990). *Tools for learning: A guide to teaching study skills.* Alexandria, VA: Association for Supervision and Curriculum Development.

Hall, G. E., Wallace R. C., & Dossett, W. A. (1973). *A Developmental conceptualization of the adoption process within educational institutions.* Austin, TX: Research and Development Center for Teacher Education, University of Texas.

Holcomb, E. L. (1999). *Getting excited about data: How to combine people, passion, and proof.* Thousand Oaks, CA: Corwin.

Kleinert, H. L., & Kearns, J. F. (2004). Alternate assessments. In F. P. Orelove, D. S. Obsey, & R. K. Siberman (Eds.), *Educating children with multiple disabilities: A collaborative approach.* Baltimore: Paul H. Brookes.

Koenig, A. J., & Rex, E. (1996). Instruction of literacy skills to children and youths with low vision. In A. L. Corn & A. J. Koenig (Eds.), *Foundations of low vision: Clinical and functional perspectives* (pp. 280–305). New York: AFB.

Levine, D. U., & Lazotte, L. W. (1990). *Unusually effective schools: A review and analysis of research and practice.* Madison, WI: National Center for Effective Schools.

Ritter, S., & Idol-Maestas, L. (1986). Teaching middle school students to use a test-taking strategy. *Journal of Educational Research, 79*(6), 350–357.

Rivera, C., Collum, E., Shafer, L., & Sia, J. K. (2004). *Analysis of state assessment policies regarding the accommodation of English language learners, SY 2000–2001.* Arlington, VA: George Washington University, Center for Equity and Excellence in Education.

Schumm, J. S., Vaughn, S., & Leavell, A. (1994). Planning pyramid: A framework for planning for diverse student needs during content area instruction. *The Reading Teacher, 47*(8), 608–615.

Scruggs, T. E., & Mastropieri, M. A. (1992). *Teaching test-taking skills: Helping students show what they know.* Cambridge, MA: Brookline Books.

Thurlow, M., Elliott, J., & Ysseldyke, J. (2003). *Testing students with disabilities: Practical strategies for complying with district and state requirements (2nd ed.).* Thousand Oaks, CA: Corwin.

Index